Grow and Cook

Grow and Cook

Tom Doorley
Johann Doorley

Gill & Macmillan

Gill & Macmillan Ltd
Hume Avenue, Park West, Dublin 12
with associated companies throughout the world
www.gillmacmillan.ie
© Tom Doorley and Johann Doorley 2007
978 07171 4163 0
Index compiled by Cover to Cover
Photography by Hugh McElveen
Food styling by Anne-Marie Tobin
Design and print origination by Design Image

This book is typeset in 11 pt Berling Roman on 18 pt leading.

The paper used in this book comes from the wood pulp of managed forests.
For every tree felled, at least one tree is planted, thereby renewing natural resources.

A CIP catalogue record for this book is available from the British Library.

1 3 5 4 2

contents

Acknowledgements   viii

Introduction   1

A Few Words of Gardening Advice   3

How We Cook   5

JANUARY

GARDEN   11

RECIPES   13

Chicken noodle soup   14

Risotto   16

Pumpkin pizza   17

Beetroot, carrot and chard stir-fry   20

Blue cheese and walnut salad   21

Chicken with 40 cloves of garlic   23

Lemon sauce pudding   24

Orange cake   25

Seville orange marmalade   26

Orangeade   29

Granny's lemonade   31

FEBRUARY

GARDEN   35

RECIPES   37

Pumpkin soup   38

Parsley and scallion omelette   39

Amarone risotto   40

Roast pumpkin with cumin, thyme and oregano   41

Potato bread   42

Toasted goat's cheese with winter salad leaves   45

Gremolata-topped fish fillets   46

Loin of bacon with parsley sauce   48

Pancakes   50

MARCH

GARDEN   53

RECIPES   55

Artichoke soup with rosemary   56

Caldo verde   59

Potatoes dauphinoise   60

Champ   61

Pumpkin and feta quiche   62

Purple sprouting broccoli and hollandaise   64

Tom's hollandaise   65

Stoved artichokes   66

Ray/skate with black butter   67

Coddle   68

APRIL

GARDEN   71

RECIPES   73

Nettle soup   74

Leeks wrapped in prosciutto   76

Amy's cheesy leek bake   78

Chicken and leek pie   79

Lamb hot pot   82

Rhubarb crumble 83

Hot cross buns 84

Rhubarb and ginger jam 86

Crystallised primroses 87

MAY

GARDEN 91

RECIPES 95

Broad bean soup 96

Cavolo nero and pine nut sauce
for pasta 97

Green salads 98

Salad dressings 99

Caesar salad 102

Beef stew with cobbler topping 103

Gooseberry and elderflower fool 105

Gooseberry jam 106

Elderflower cordial 109

JUNE

GARDEN 113

RECIPES 115

Pea and mint soup 116

Byessar 117

Risotto primavera 118

Courgette and herb frittata 120

Herby new potato salad 121

Potato salad with radish and
capers 123

Mayonnaise 123

Lamb kebabs 124

Summer birthday cake 127

Strawberry jam 128

JULY

GARDEN 131

RECIPES 133

Gazpacho 134

Tomato salad #1 135

Tomato salad #2 136

Cucumber salad 137

Tomato and cucumber salad 138

Fresh tomato sauce 138

Tzatziki 139

Globe artichokes 140

Salad Niçoise 141

Barbecue 142

Redcurrant tartlets 144

Blackcurrant jam 146

AUGUST

GARDEN 149

RECIPES 151

Roast tomatoes 152

Roast tomato and celery soup 154

Vegetable fritters 155

Aubergines with pesto 157

Tomato salsa 158

Bolognese 159

Field mushroom sauce 161

Plums with hazelnut crumble 162

Plum jam 164

SEPTEMBER

GARDEN 167

RECIPES 169

French onion soup 170

Crostini 171

Aubergine Parmigiano 173

Aubergine and yoghurt purée 175

Smoked haddock supper 176

Lamb arm stew 177

Onion and goat's cheese pizza 178

Blackberry and apple pie 180

Raspberry jam 182

Elderberry chutney 184

OCTOBER

GARDEN 187

RECIPES 189

Celeriac soup 190

Pumpkin filo pastry parcels 191

Gem Store squashes with
tarragon cream 192

Waldorf salad 194

Hake with stewed peppers 195

Roast beef, roast spuds and
horseradish sauce 196

Yorkshire pudding 199

Shepherd's pie 200

Christmas mincemeat 201

Beetroot cake 202

Blackberry and apple jam 204

Sloe gin 207

NOVEMBER

GARDEN 211

RECIPES 212

Beetroot soup 213

Beetroot and orange salad 214

Celeriac remoulade 216

Colcannon 217

New World coddle 219

Chard and feta flatbreads 220

Stir-fried chard 222

Roast pork belly with
Chinese spices 224

DECEMBER

GARDEN 227

RECIPES 228

Leek and potato soup 229

Red cabbage and apple 230

Carrot and ginger salad 232

Roast root vegetables 233

Brussels sprouts 234

Roast goose 235

Potted goose 239

Mince pies 240

Profiteroles 242

Index 245

Acknowledgements

While this book is dedicated to the memory of our mothers, Johann would like to mention the encouragement and patience of Delia Reilly who helped her to learn to cook and to appreciate good food.

We would like to thank our daughters Sarah, Georgia and Roberta for their help in the kitchen, as we tested and tasted these recipes, and in the garden where they were united in their enthusiasm for baby carrots.

We would like to thank Fergal Tobin at Gill & Macmillan for combining several of our ideas and refining them into this book.

We also want to record our gratitude to Sarah Liddy and all the team at Gill & Macmillan for guiding this project into print.

Finally, many thanks to Hugh McElveen for the photographs and to Anne Marie Tobin for the food styling. And to both for their description of Johann's pastry as photogenic!

Dedication

IN MEMORY OF OUR MOTHERS

ETHEL MCKEEVER
1922–2006

AND

ANITA DOORLEY
1921–1991

introduction

The idea behind this book was very simple. We wanted to give an account of what we eat at home and how we cook it. Of course, it soon became apparent that we would have to do more than that, because so much of what ends up in our kitchen has come all the way from the garden, a matter of about 120 metres.

And so, this book has ended up being about growing and cooking. But don't let that put you off. There is nothing, absolutely nothing, as good as fruit and vegetables that have been picked only minutes before they appear on the table. And the sense of satisfaction in turning the contents of a seed packet into a meal, or part of a meal, is something that you have to experience for yourself.

The good news is that growing your own is actually very easy. What it requires is essentially time, patience and some degree of elbow grease. But it can be done, perhaps in a window box. Growing your own mustard and cress or sprouting your own seeds doesn't even require that. And it's a start.

But even if you never buy a packet of seeds, we hope you will use and enjoy *Grow and Cook* because freshness and good ingredients don't have to come from your own garden and the sweat of your brow. It's all about eating with the seasons and cutting down, as far as possible, on food miles. If you see nothing wrong, or at least strange, in eating asparagus from Peru or raspberries from California, you probably just won't get it. But if you support local organic growers (and sometimes wonder what the hell you do with cavolo nero or celeriac), we reckon you will.

And let's not get too doctrinaire about all this. There's nothing wrong with a few Spanish peppers or Italian aubergines during the Hungry Gap in late spring. And let's face it, there's no such thing as a local mango. No, what this book is all about is good food, carefully but simply prepared, in a way that lets the raw materials speak for themselves. We are not into cheffy food.

In this part of the world, we don't have much tradition of treating vegetables with respect. The plant element in the standard 'meat and three veg' is there as an afterthought, a kind of bulking agent. And these days, when we are all told to eat more vegetables because of their health benefits, there's still precious little talk of how good they can taste if they aren't cooked to perdition. For too long, vegetables have been seen as a penance. We are hoping to highlight the potential pleasure.

Fresh produce from the supermarket, the farmers' market or the local independent greengrocer is often fresh and very good, but don't expect something that was picked weeks ago in a far-off land to taste as good as its local equivalent. If your vegetables carry only wellie metres rather than air miles or road miles, you'll be getting the real thing, the full blast of flavour and the full complement of nutrients.

If you do decide to try growing your own, grow what you want. Don't grow things because you feel you should (we have never grown cauliflower, for example). But it's good to experiment and you may discover a taste for vegetables that you never encountered before. What about scorzonera? Or kohlrabi? There's lots of scope.

If you have decided to eat more vegetables but don't really enjoy them much, give it time. Grow and eat as widely as possible, swap crops with friends, and in time you'll wonder how you could have overlooked so much pleasure for so long.

But be aware of some things. Heritage and 'heirloom' varieties don't always taste better. Brand new F^1 hybrids can be delicious and better suited to organic growing. Lots of manure is almost always a good thing. Regular hoeing is by far the best way to keep down weeds. Digging is good exercise.

And vegetable growing is addictive. What starts as a few herbs on the windowsill can end up as a full-blown allotment habit.

In any case, while we would love to think that this book will encourage people to sow or plant something edible, what we really want is for you to enjoy cooking and eating the recipes that we have collected here. They are our favourites and we hope they become yours too.

Johann and Tom Doorley

Carrigeen Hill

Co. Cork

Summer 2007

a few words of gardening advice

It's amazing how much in the way of fresh vegetables you can grow without a great deal of effort. Even really lazy gardening gets results, even if the result is not quite perfect.

Weeds do actually compete with crops, so keeping them down is not just a question of neatness. Hand weeding and hoeing will actually give you bigger, better and healthier veg.

The soil needs feeding and the best food is rotted manure or compost because the organic matter not only delivers plant nutrients, it also helps to create the right kind of soil texture for happy roots.

The average household with an average garden will never be able to produce enough compost to sustain a busy vegetable plot, but making compost is still worthwhile. Getting in farmyard or stable manure is pretty well essential if you want to grow lots. Just make sure that it's not fresh. Manure needs to rot down for at least three months before it goes into the soil; otherwise it may scorch your precious plants and, oddly enough, steal nitrogen from the soil to help with its decomposition.

The precise depth for sowing seeds and spacing for plants is important and the best source of information about this is to be found on seed packets. The seed companies know best how their particular varieties should be grown.

Whether or not you use chemicals in the garden is up to you. We avoid them wherever possible because we find they aren't really necessary and because we like our produce and the local wildlife to be untainted. We also avoid synthetic fertilizers because the soil, if it's kept in good shape, shouldn't need any further assistance. But we don't like to be preachy about this.

After all, the world would be a better place if more people grew at least some of what they eat, however they go about it.

how we cook

cookers

When we first married, we were given a gas cooker as a wedding present, but now we have a two-oven Aga and a Baby Belling. In total, we have cooked on gas for nineteen years, electricity for one year and with an Aga for just over two years so far. We therefore think in gas marks, but have quickly become adept at thinking of oven positions for the Aga. The temperature of the roasting oven ranges between GM5/190°C/375°F in the centre to GM8/230°C/450°F right at the top or on the floor. How much the hot plates have been in use also affects the heat of the roasting oven. Checking the position of the mercury on the Aga has become second nature. The simmering oven temperature is about the same as GM3/170°C/340°F – hot enough to cook things slowly, but cool enough to heat serving plates. The Aga also heats our water and because it is on all the time gives us background heat throughout the house. The Baby Belling is electric and has an oven, a grill and two rings. Before we got the Aga, we cooked supper for fourteen with it.

meat

We buy fresh beef and lamb from our local butcher, who has his own farm and slaughterhouse. We also get fresh pork from him, but he buys in the pigs. Bacon and rashers are 'Quality Assured' from the supermarket. We also buy frozen organic beef direct from a local farm where fresh organic chickens and eggs are sold. They also have organic turkeys and geese for Christmas.

fish

We live half an hour's drive from the sea but have found that the quality of fresh fish available has become variable. We eat less fish than we probably should to keep the nutritionists happy, but with fish stocks falling and little or no consensus between the fishing industry, the EU and the scientists, perhaps we should give it up altogether or our grandchildren may never taste cod.

5

dairy

Milk and butter are Irish from the local co-op. Cream and yoghurt are an Irish organic brand from the supermarket. Cheese is mostly local, extending as far as Wexford for cheddar and the occasional piece of Stilton at Christmas.

oil

We have supermarket own-brand extra virgin olive oil, organic sunflower oil, toasted sesame oil and occasionally treat ourselves to a bottle of special extra virgin olive oil.

tins

A few tins each of organic tomatoes, organic chickpeas and Ortiz tuna are kept in the press. Sometimes spaghetti hoops, organic baked beans and tomato soup are spotted there too.

pasta and rice

Pasta is so cheap it is worth paying a little more for a good brand, particularly the egg pastas. We keep penne rigate, tagliatelle, spaghetti and lasagne in stock. Oriental noodles are useful too – we like buckwheat soba noodles, mung bean noodles and spinach and egg 'three-minute' noodles. White and brown basmati rice are also staples, as well as carnaroli or arborio for risottos. A bag of bulgur and a bag of couscous usually end up in the cupboard with the pastas and rice.

seeds and pulses

Sesame, sunflower and pumpkin seeds, pine nuts, walnuts, almonds and hazelnuts are all used regularly. A stock of dried orange lentils, puy lentils and chickpeas can be found there too.

seasonings

Sea salt, both fine and coarse, sits in an enamel container beside the Aga. How much salt you use is a matter of taste. The quantity of salt added to each dish is up to you, except when making bread. Bread needs salt to taste and some is also necessary to improve the texture of yeast breads, but feel free to adjust the amount. We have a grinder of coarse salt on the table too. Black pepper is also kept in a grinder beside the Aga as well as on the table.

The spices we use most are whole coriander, cumin, cardamom, cinnamon, nutmeg and dark mustard seed. In addition, we use ground turmeric, ginger, Chinese five spice, paprika and cinnamon.

Fresh ginger is always in the vegetable rack, along with onions, shallots and garlic.

Soy sauce, Worcestershire sauce, Tabasco sauce, mango chutney and lime pickle complete the stores.

freezer

We have to admit to keeping a bag of peas in there. They are the one thing that freeze really well and Birds Eye do it best. We use the freezer to store surplus from the garden for later use. We also store meat and chicken in it to save on trips to the butcher or the farm during the school holidays.

larder and shed

The larder has two outside walls and four vents to keep it cool. This is very effective in winter and okay in summer. It has no natural light, so it's perfect for storing potatoes. It's where we store our jam, marmalade, lemonade, sloe gin and onions, etc.

Apples, squashes, pumpkins and onions are all stored in the shed and brought into the larder as needed.

flour

We use an organic strong white flour, an organic fine whole wheat flour and cream or plain white flour for baking.

Why no cauliflower in the book? Apart from the fact that Johann can't spell it ('coliflower'), Tom doesn't really like it and we haven't got round to growing it, but we might yet.

january

garden

Just as there are pessimists and optimists, there are two schools of thought about the month of January. Some of us find it a bit of an anticlimax as life returns to its more mundane rhythms after the excitement of Christmas. Others see the New Year as a fresh start bursting with opportunities. We often find ourselves somewhere in between.

This is certainly a month for planning ahead if you're concerned about growing your own vegetables. Above all, it's a time for relatively simple, cleansing and comforting food.

In the kitchen, we find ourselves turning to dishes like chicken noodle soup as an antidote to the feasting of Christmas. But there's plenty of scope for heartier food too, like when we return from the great but often cold and wet outdoors to a slow-cooked one-pot dish like lamb hotpot bubbling away gently in the slow oven of the Aga. Pot-roasted chicken with masses and masses of garlic, gobbled up with plenty of fresh, crusty bread, feels positively therapeutic.

If, like us, you want to use as much fresh, local or home-grown produce as possible, you might see January as a rather bleak month. The low temperatures and short days are certainly not conducive to growth, but this is not yet the Hungry Gap. That will come later in the year.

There is a still lot of good stuff from the previous growing season. There are root vegetables and colourful squashes and pumpkins in storage (at their most fragrant just now) and salad crops, sown in the late summer, are still providing plenty of greenery. Bright, multicoloured chard stalks are still braving the elements in the open air and the leeks, those amazingly nutritious and hardy things, are coming to their peak. Winter cabbage, sprouts and their Italian cousin, the wonderful cavolo nero, have developed a lovely sweetness thanks to the frosts. The best of the European citrus fruits (as local as these things go) are coming into the shops and bringing with them their hoarded sunshine.

This is the traditional time for marmalade making, a process that fills the whole house with a sunny, summery, citrus aroma in the depths of winter. But there's a great deal more to oranges and lemons than that.

For us, this is also a time for studying the seed catalogues, which is one of the most satisfying forms of armchair gardening, especially if you do it beside a warm fire as the winter winds howl outside.

Beyond the armchair, there is work to be done in the garden. Digging, to turn over the soil and maybe incorporate some manure, is a big job and best done on a little-and-often basis. The plan should be to have the vegetable garden ready for action by the time the first early potatoes go in, if you are to follow the ancient Irish tradition, around St Patrick's Day. But like many plans, this one can easily go astray. Turning over the soil on a bad day in January can lead to thoughts of emigration.

However, taking the optimistic line, things can only get better and it's essential to be prepared. Sowing seeds of tomatoes, peppers and aubergines in early January is a symbol of hope. It also makes very sound sense in a climate where such tender crops need as much time as possible to reach fruition.

We sow ours, in modules, on the kitchen window ledge where high-performance double glazing keeps out the frost, and the Aga, an essential piece of kit for us, keeps the temperature nice and balmy. As February arrives, often with the worst weather of the year, the seedlings are putting out their first true leaves. Little do they know what it's like outside, but by April, having been potted on, they will have reached an impressive height of a foot or so and the first tiny flower buds appear with the promise of tasty fruit for the summer.

All in all, January is a satisfying month.

recipes

January is an official beginning of the year, as the seasons run in a continuous cycle, flowing smoothly from one into the next. With the hustle and bustle of Christmas over, it's good to take stock of what grew well the previous year and how much of each crop we would like this year. It's also a good time for planting trees and clearing dead branches from the woods.

This is a good time to tidy the larder in preparation for the fresh pots of marmalade. The smell of marmalade being made is very cleansing, driving out the stale winter air from the house.

chicken noodle soup

Serves 4

A perfectly fine stock can be made from the remains of a roast chicken, but the best jellied stock is made from the leftover bones and cartilage after we've had a tray of roasted chicken wings. Boiled up, strained and left to cool in the fridge, it can be cut with a knife into slices. Used in the chicken noodle soup, it leaves your lips sticky and your tummy warm with ginger. Perfect for a regular after-school lunch in the winter months.

Spicy chicken stock

1 roast chicken carcass or
   remains of 8 roasted chicken
   wings
1 small carrot, sliced
1 stick of celery, chopped
1 onion and its skin, sliced
2 cloves of garlic, chopped
knob of ginger, peeled and grated
stick of lemongrass, chopped
chilli, as much or as little as you
   like, chopped
1 bay leaf
1 tsp salt and black pepper
1 tbsp soy sauce
1 tsp nam pla (Thai fish sauce)
1 litre (1¾ pints) water

Put everything into a pot and bring to the boil. Cover and simmer on the lowest heat possible or place in the bottom oven of the Aga at approx. GM2/150°C/300°F for 2 hours. When done, strain the stock through a sieve.

Soup

1 onion

2 cloves of garlic

piece of fresh ginger, about the size
of a wine cork

2 tbsp sunflower oil

1 leek or bunch of greens, cabbage
or chard, whatever is in the
garden

1 carrot

3 tbsp sweetcorn

1 litre (1¾ pints) spicy stock (above)

2 tbsp soy sauce

2 blocks of 4-minute noodles

Peel the onion, then halve and thinly slice it into rings. Peel
and thinly slice the garlic. Peel the ginger and cut into fine
sticks.

Heat the oil in a saucepan on a low heat and add the onion,
garlic and ginger. While they are softening in the oil, clean and
shred the leek or greens and cut the carrot into thin sticks.
Add to the onions. (If you are using stalks of chard, they can
be cut into thin sticks and added to the onions first to soften a
little.)

Mix and add the sweetcorn, stock and soy sauce. Bring to the
boil, then add the noodles. Stir and simmer for 4 minutes.

Serve with chopsticks, kitchen paper and spoons. Slurping is
good!

risotto

Serves 4–6

This is Tom's speciality and a great way to show off a small quantity of choice vegetables. All it needs is a salad to follow. Perfect for a lazy weekend lunch or a quick supper after a busy day.

It is the nearest thing to convenience food we do, as there is always stock in the freezer and something growing in the garden. Peas are a freezer staple and there are always a few rashers or a packet of smoked bacon bits in the fridge.

850 ml (1½ pints) stock
2 tbsp olive oil
125 g (4 oz) smoked bacon, cut into small bits
285 g (10 oz) carnaroli rice
200 ml (7 fl oz) dry white wine
bunch of scallions or a medium leek or some greens from the garden, finely sliced
85 g (3 oz) peas
60 g (2 oz) parmesan, grated
30 g (1 oz) butter
salt and pepper

Put the stock in a pot and keep hot. Heat the oil in a deep, wide frying pan and add the bacon bits. Cook over a moderate heat until the bits begin to go brown and crispy.

Scoop out the bacon bits, leaving the fat. Add the rice to the pan and coat it well with the fat, turn the heat up and add the wine. Bubble for a minute to evaporate the alcohol. Stir. Turn down the heat to a moderate simmer – not too slow. Keep stirring.

When the rice is just starting to stick, add a ladle of hot stock. Keep stirring. As each ladleful is absorbed, add another. Keep stirring. Different types of rice need more or less liquid. Keep stirring. The rice is done when it looks translucent and the chalky bit has gone from the middle. Keep stirring. Start tasting about 15 minutes after the wine goes in.

As soon as the rice is done, add the greens, bacon and peas. Stir them through for a minute and take off the heat. Add the cheese and butter and stir.

pumpkin pizza

Serves 4

Pumpkins store well in a cool place, and around this time of year they smell of ripe melon when cut open. Their bright colour and sunny smell brighten the darkest of January days. Feta cheese works well on this pizza and any leftover pumpkin is easily turned into soup.

1 level tsp dried yeast

$1/4$ tsp sugar

280 ml (10 fl oz) hand-hot water

1 tsp salt

450 g (1 lb) strong white flour

1 small pumpkin, about 400 g (14 oz) prepared

1 tub of soft goat's cheese (120 g/ $4^1/2$ oz) – we like Ardsallagh

thyme leaves

salt, pepper and olive oil

Mix the yeast, sugar and some of the warm water in a cup and leave in a warm place to froth. (I find the front of the Aga between the lids is perfect.) Add the salt to the rest of the water and keep warm.

Weigh the flour and sieve into a bowl. (Warm the bowl first if your house is on the cool side.)

The yeast is ready when it has a head like a pint of stout. Pour the yeast into the flour, rinse out the cup with some of the warm water and pour into the flour, adding the rest of the water. Flours vary in the amount of water they need; you may need more or less than the amount given.

Mix in the water and start to knead the dough, either in a mixer with a dough hook or by hand. Keep kneading until the dough is smooth and springy.

Take the dough out and pour a tablespoon of oil into the bowl. Put the dough back into the bowl and smear it with the

oil. Cover and leave to rise. The time taken to rise depends on temperature – 60–90 minutes when somewhere warm, or all day if somewhere cooler. When the dough has doubled in size and has a domed top, it is ready to use.

Switch the oven to its highest setting and place a flat baking sheet on the rack in the hottest part of the oven.

Divide the dough into 4 balls, dust with flour and set aside (they need a rest before shaping).

Peel and deseed the pumpkin and cut into thin slices about 2 mm ($\frac{1}{8}$ inch) thick.

Take a ball of dough and gently squeeze and stretch it out into a circle of about 26 cm (10 inches) in diameter. Put the dough onto a floured baking sheet with no edges and cover the centre with a single layer of pumpkin slices, leaving a 1 cm ($\frac{1}{2}$ inch) edge. Dot with teaspoonfuls of goat's cheese and sprinkle with some thyme, salt, pepper and a dribble of olive oil.

Shake the baking sheet gently to get the pizza to move, then slide the pizza onto the baking sheet in the oven. Be brave – the thicker the dough base, the easier it is. Close the oven door and make the next pizza, by which time the first pizza will be almost ready. It may need to be turned for even cooking. Slide out the cooked pizza using a long fish slice and slide in the next pizza. Keep sharing the pizzas as they come out of the oven.

beetroot, carrot and chard stir-fry

Serves 4–6

The first time we had this was one Sunday lunch when the vegetable plot seemed particularly bare, and as an all-in-one vegetable dish it did the job extremely well. Adding some prawns, tofu cubes or beef strips after the onion, etc. makes this a one-pot meal.

1 beetroot

2 carrots

4 large chard leaves

1 small chilli

1 cm (½ inch) piece of fresh ginger

3 tbsp oil

1 onion, peeled, halved and sliced

2 cloves of garlic, peeled and sliced

2 tbsp soy sauce

Scrub the beetroot and cut into quarters. Place in a steamer for 20 minutes. Peel the carrots and cut into narrow strips 6 cm (2 inches) long and steam.

Wash the chard leaves and remove the green leafy part from the mid-ribs. Cut the mid-ribs across into narrow strips. If the green leafy part of the chard is not too moth-eaten, dry it in a salad spinner and cut it into thin ribbons.

Cut the chilli open, remove the seeds and cut into thin slices. Peel and grate the ginger.

When the beetroot is tender, remove from the steamer. Peel and cut into long thin strips like the carrot.

Heat the oil in a large frying pan or wok over a high heat. Add the onion, garlic, chilli and ginger to the oil. Stir for a minute and add the carrot, beetroot and chard mid-ribs. When they are all hot and beginning to sizzle, stir well and add the chard leaf ribbons. Pop the lid on for 2–3 minutes and then add the soy sauce. Stir for a minute or two and serve when hot.

blue cheese and walnut salad

Serves 2 as a light meal or 4 as a small starter

Blue cheese and walnuts in their shells are a must for Christmas. We like Crozier best, but will happily eat Cashel blue or Stilton. Fresh walnuts in their shells are far nicer than packets from the shop, and cracking them open is always a gamble. If you only have packet walnuts, toast them lightly in a dry pan over a medium heat for 5 minutes or so to improve their flavour.

Picking winter salad leaves, including lambs lettuce, rocket, winter purslane, landcress and parsley, in the polytunnel on a bright winter's day is a good feeling and they taste great.

We eat this salad as part of a meal with soup and bread or as a salad starter.

60 g (2 oz) winter salad leaves

60 g (2 oz) blue cheese

8 walnuts, shelled and broken into pieces

1 shallot

4 tbsp light olive oil

1 tsp walnut oil

1 tbsp lemon juice

Wash the salad leaves and dry well. Put them in a salad bowl. Crumble the cheese into small pieces over the salad leaves and add the walnut pieces. Just before serving, peel and slice the shallot as thinly as possible and sprinkle the shallot rings over the salad. Dress the salad with the oils and lemon juice, toss and serve.

chicken with 40 cloves of garlic

Serves 4–6

Yes, 40 cloves of garlic at least! As there are 10–15 cloves to a bulb, you will need 4 bulbs.

1 chicken 1 kg 800 g (4 lb)
40 cloves of garlic
glass of white wine
bunch of fresh herbs
3 tbsp olive oil

Paste
110 g (4 oz) plain flour
1 tsp salt
4–5 tbsp water

Heat the oven to GM5/190°C/375°F.

Leave the garlic in its skin and divide into cloves, then spread them over the bottom of a casserole. Put the herbs inside the chicken and place it on top of the garlic. Pour the glass of wine and the olive oil over the chicken.

To make the paste, mix the flour and salt, and add enough water to make a soft dough. Roll the dough/paste into a long sausage. Wet the edge of the casserole and lay the sausage of dough/paste on it. The sausage needs to go all the way around. Wet the top of the dough/paste and put the lid on the casserole. This seals in the chicken.

Put the sealed casserole into the oven and cook for 2 hours.

Bring the sealed casserole to the table and open; the scent of the garlic and the chicken is amazing. The chicken will be tender and evenly browned; the cloves of garlic soft and spreadable. All it needs is lots of bread and salad to go with it, and a glass or two of wine.

lemon sauce pudding

Serves 6

This is quick and easy to make and lemons are so good at this time of year. We sometimes use Seville oranges when they are in season during January as a variation instead of the lemons.

145 g (5 oz) butter
260 g (9 oz) sugar
5 eggs, separated
75 g (2½ oz) plain flour, sieved
grated rind and juice of 2½ lemons
300 ml (½ pint) milk

Set the oven to GM4/180°C/350°F. Boil the kettle and butter a 1.5 litre (3 pint) ovenproof dish.

Cream the butter and sugar together until pale and beat in the egg yolks. Stir in the flour, lemon rind, juice and milk in that order.

Whisk the egg whites until stiff and fold into the mixture, then pour into the buttered dish and stand in a roasting tin.

Pour boiling water into the tin around the dish and put the tin into the oven to bake for 35–40 minutes, until the sponge topping is golden and feels firm in the middle. It will look like lemon curd underneath the sponge. Serve with lightly whipped cream.

orange cake

A slice of cake and a cup of tea in the afternoon are welcome treats, and with oranges being so good during this month, they are worth taking advantage of. If we could grow citrus fruits, we would, but then we wouldn't have the climate to grow apples!

Cake
170 g (6 oz) soft butter
170 g (6 oz) caster sugar
3 eggs
170 g (6 oz) self-raising flour
1 level tsp baking powder
1 orange, organic or unwaxed

Set the oven to GM4/180°C/350°F. Line two round shallow cake tins 18 cm (7 inches) in diameter with buttered parchment paper.

Cut up the butter into a mixing bowl with the sugar and eggs. Sift in the flour and baking powder. Finely grate most of the orange zest into the mixing bowl, saving a heaped teaspoonful for the icing.

Beat together the contents of the bowl until smooth and creamy. Divide the mixture between the two cake tins and bake for 20–30 minutes in the centre of the oven.

The cakes are done when they spring back when gently poked with a finger. Take them out of the oven and remove from the tins onto a wire rack. Peel off the paper and leave to cool.

Icing
85 g (3 oz) soft butter
230 g (8 oz) icing sugar
2 tbsp orange juice

Put the butter into a bowl and sift in the icing sugar. Add the juice of half the orange and the reserved grated orange zest. Beat well until pale and creamy.

Spread half the icing over one of the cooled cakes, then place the other cake on top and cover with the remaining icing.

seville orange marmalade

Makes 12–14 pots

The following hints and tips can be applied to all the recipes for jams, jellies and chutney in this book.

- Use only fresh, good-quality, unblemished fruit. Fruit that is just ripe is best, as it contains pectin in its most usable form and therefore sets better. If you want a really stiff jam, use some under-ripe fruit, but we tend to have ours a bit runny.

- Jams, jellies and marmalades should be made in small quantities. The mix will reach setting point more quickly and will preserve the colour and quality of the fruit. It is also quicker and less laborious.

- Use dry fruit – preserves made from wet fruit (especially soft berry fruits) are more likely to grow mould. When we use frozen fruit, we put it straight into the pan without defrosting it first.

- A wide, deep saucepan is best, as the mix comes to the boil, and will reach setting point, more quickly.

- Sugar must be completely dissolved before the preserve comes to the boil, otherwise it will crystallise upon cooling. Warmed sugar dissolves more quickly; it can be warmed in the oven before the jars go in to be sterilised.

- To test preserves for the setting point, either use a sugar thermometer or carry out a wrinkle test. When the setting point has been reached, the sugar thermometer should reach 105°C/220°F. To do the wrinkle test, put a teaspoonful of preserve from the pot onto a cool plate. Leave to cool in the fridge for a minute or two. When cool, push the edge of the preserve with your finger. If the surface wrinkles, it has reached the setting point. We use the wrinkle test.

●   Jars for preserves must be spotlessly clean and sterilised. We remove all labels, wash them in hot soapy water and rinse them. Then we sterilise them in the simmering oven of the Aga or you can use a warm oven (GM1/140°C/285°F) for 20 minutes before use. If we use screw top jars, we pop in the metal lids too.

Safety

●   The setting point of jam is approximately 105°C/220°F, so it can burn badly. It's a good idea to wear oven gloves while stirring and to make sure the saucepan is big enough so that the mixture does not splash out. When potting jam, take care: use a heatproof measuring jug to fill the jars.

Never pour from the saucepan into the jars or you could get scalded. To prevent the glass jars cracking, a knife may be placed in each one before pouring in the jam. We leave the jars in the oven until the jam is ready to be potted up so that we are pouring the cooled jam into hot jars.

My mother's marathon marmalade-making sessions kept us well supplied for the year, as well as having enough pots to give away. Ours are on a more modest scale and the mincer attachment on the Kenwood makes short work of shredding the peel. However, doing this over two days is less laborious.

The flavour of the first fresh pot is like no other in the batch.

1.4 kg (3 lb) Seville oranges

2 lemons

3.4 litres (6 pints) water

2.7 kg (6 lb) sugar

14 jam jars and covers

Wash the oranges and lemons, cut in halves and squeeze the juice out. Collect the pips and pulp into a muslin bag. Chop or mince the orange and lemon peels and put into a large pot with the water and juice. Tie up the muslin bag and put it into the pot. Leave overnight.

Have 14 very clean glass jars (see p. 27) ready on a baking tray.

Bring the pot to the boil and simmer for about 2 hours, until the peel is soft. It should feel like 'bread and milk' between your fingers. Do make sure the peel is soft, because once you add the sugar, it won't soften any more.

The liquid will have reduced by about half. Take out the muslin bag and squeeze it between two plates to get out all the pectin.

Add the sugar and stir until all of it has dissolved, then bring to the boil. Boil fast for about 15 minutes and test for the setting point (see pp. 26–7). While the rest is cooling, put the clean jam pots into the oven at GM1/140°C/285°F to sterilise.

Stir in a knob of butter to disperse the froth. Take the pot off the heat and leave to cool for 15 minutes.

Use a small heatproof jug to fill the hot jam pots and cover the marmalade with waxed discs, smooth side down. Wipe the jars and cover with damp cellophane held in place with rubber bands. Leave to cool. Store in a cool, dry larder.

orangeade

Makes approx. 1.45 litres (2½ pints) of concentrate

Based on our basic lemonade recipe, this tastes like liquid marmalade. If you make it at the same time as the marmalade, add the extra pips and pulp from this recipe to the muslin bag.

450 g (1 lb) sugar
3 large Seville oranges
1.15 litres (2 pints) water

Put the sugar into a bowl and using a sharp knife or a potato peeler, pare the zest from the oranges, taking as little of the white pith as you can. Add the zest to the sugar and boil the kettle.

Squeeze the juice from the oranges and add to the sugar and zest. Pour in the boiling water and stir until the sugar has dissolved. Cover the bowl with a plate or cling film and leave overnight.

Strain the orangeade from the zest and bottle. Drink diluted to taste.

granny's lemonade

Makes two 700 ml (1¼ pints) bottles

We make this all year round, but with lemons at their best in the winter, I sometimes make extra and freeze it in three-quarters-full plastic bottles for later in the year.

3 lemons, unwaxed or preferably organic
450 g (1 lb) sugar
1 level tsp citric acid
850 ml (1½ pints) boiling water

Using a sharp knife or potato peeler, thinly peel the rind from the lemons, taking as little of the white pith as you can, and put in a big bowl. Squeeze the lemons and add the juice to the bowl, then add the sugar, citric acid and finally the boiling water. Stir until the sugar has dissolved. Cover the bowl with a plate or some cling film and leave overnight.

The next day, strain the lemonade and bottle it. Dilute to taste; we like a ratio of about 1 part lemonade to 3 parts water. This concentrate makes a very credible alcopop if you add vodka, but make sure you know which jug is which, or the children might get hold of it.

february

garden

Contrary to what T.S. Eliot says, February is the cruellest month. If it is not very, very wet for days on end, it will deliver several consecutive nights of hard frost or the wind will turn bitterly cold. Or a rather depressing blend of all these conditions.

February is definitely a month to spend inside and if, like us, you have a polytunnel, or even a greenhouse, there is something very pleasant about being able to defy the elements, even if you still have to wrap up in multiple layers of clothing.

We like to sow some spuds in the polytunnel as early as we can. According to the old gardening books, you could get seed potatoes shortly after Christmas in days gone by. These days, they tend not to appear in the garden centres until the end of January at the earliest.

As soon as we can get our hands on them, we buy our spuds for sprouting. All you have to do is place them in boxes (egg boxes are great because they hold the tubers upright) with the 'rose' end uppermost (this is the part of the potato with the most 'eyes').

Sprouting, or chitting, potatoes is very simple. Having arranged them as above, you need to keep the tubers in a cool but frost-free place where they can get a reasonable amount of light. After a couple of weeks you will notice the eyes starting to grow and by the time you plant them, ideally at the end of March, the little sprouts will be quite sturdy. If you look carefully, you'll be able to see tiny roots starting to form at their bases.

Traditionally, most gardeners grew early potatoes on the basis that the main crop varieties, the ones that are used throughout the winter, were relatively cheap. These days, there are other considerations, such as space. Main crops need more room, they occupy the ground for ages and they are prone to blight.

We have the room to grow such potatoes, but there's a great deal of work involved in spud self-sufficiency. Our current policy is to plant enough of a main crop to keep us going until Christmas, then we simply buy local organic potatoes until the first earlies are available from the garden.

And the very first of them, as I say, are planted in the polytunnel as early as possible, which usually means the first week in February. We don't bother to sprout them; they are simply planted about six inches deep and a foot apart with a good spadeful of compost or rotted manure. All going well, these first new potatoes should be on our plates by the first week in May.

There are lots of varieties to choose from, but we tend to stick with the old favourites: Home Guard, Duke of York and Sharpe's Express, or one of the newer sorts, such as Orla.

Sowing a mixture of cut-and-come-again lettuce and perhaps some rocket is the other signal task for February in the polytunnel. This involves preparing a square metre of soil with some organic matter and maybe a handful of fish, blood and bonemeal, and broadcasting the seed fairly thickly on the surface. We then cover it with a thin layer of sieved potting compost because our soil is quite stony and we want the tiny seedlings to have an easy emergence. We can harvest the first small leaves by April and the lettuce plants will continue producing lots of green stuff until they start to run to seed in the early summer. Even then, there's nothing wrong with 'bolted' lettuce, although some people find it a little bitter.

A sowing of early carrots (we use one of the Nantes varieties) done now may produce finger-sized morsels by May, but if the weather outside is very cold and dull, germination may take weeks. But it's worth the little effort involved.

Our best peas always seem to come from a February sowing in the polytunnel. We choose a hardy, early variety like Feltham First and sow a bit more densely than it advises on the packet. This is because early sowings, even under cover, are risky and because we often have to contend with the predations of mice. If all goes well, we have peas and new potatoes before the end of May.

We sow nothing outside during February except a couple of rows of broad beans, and if the weather is particularly cold, wet and miserable, they may simply rot in the ground before they get a chance to germinate. Only the hardiest varieties have any chance at this time of year and our stalwart is Claudia Aquadulce. They seem to grow best when sown six inches apart and an inch or two deep in staggered rows with a couple of feet between them. If they don't come up, we will have wasted maybe an hour's labour in the garden, but if they succeed, we will have a very tasty crop in early June.

recipes

February tends to bring the coldest weather, so we eat warming food based on the store cupboard. The polytunnel will still have parsley and salads, and outside there will be leeks, cabbage, early broccoli and some beetroot. The last of the pumpkins in storage will have to be used up.

It's a good month to take stock of what's in the freezer and start to use what's there, and in particular make jam from the stored fruit. Making something special for a Valentine's night dinner at home helps to brighten this bleak month. Pancakes are also a must on Shrove Tuesday.

pumpkin soup

Serves 4–6

Having a pot of soup ready, either to heat up or in the simmering oven, when we get in from the garden or the school run in the afternoon is very comforting. Served with some bread and cheese, it will keep hunger at bay until the evening.

50 g (2 oz) butter

1 large onion, peeled and sliced

1 kg (2 lb) pumpkin flesh, peeled and chopped

300 ml (10 fl oz) stock

1 tsp salt

pepper

170 ml (6 fl oz) cream

Vegetable stock is quick to make: combine 1 stick of chopped celery, 1 chopped carrot, 1 chopped onion with its skin and roots removed, 2 squashed garlic cloves, 1 bay leaf, $\frac{1}{2}$ tsp salt and a few grinds of black pepper to 600 ml (1 pint) of water and bring to the boil. Simmer for 15–20 minutes.

Heat the butter in a saucepan and add the onion. Stir well and cook on a medium heat until the onion is soft, then add the pumpkin and stock. Bring to the boil and gently cook until the pumpkin is soft.

Let the soup cool or add some cold water or stock, then purée. Transfer to a clean pot. If it's too thick, add some water to achieve the required consistency. Season to taste. Bring back to the boil. Before serving, add the cream in a swirl.

parsley and scallion omelette

Omelettes are so easy, they should be a compulsory requirement for the Leaving Cert. Not only are they easy, they are far cheaper than even the cheapest special offer ready-meal and only take minutes to make. We like to serve an orange and landcress salad after this omelette for a quick meal.

Per person:
2 eggs
salt and pepper
20 g (1 oz) knob of butter
2 scallions, chopped
1 tbsp parsley, chopped

Warm a plate. Break the eggs into a bowl with 1 tbsp of cold water and mix the yolks gently into the whites. Season the eggs with salt and pepper. Put the butter into a 24 cm (9 inch) omelette pan or non-stick frying pan and put over a moderate heat. When the butter melts and froths, tip the pan so that it is covered evenly with the melted butter.

Pour in the eggs and sprinkle them with the chopped scallions and parsley. With a fork, draw the edges of the omelette into the centre of the pan while tipping the pan to let the liquid egg run to the edges. When the egg is no longer liquid but still soft, fold the omelette in half and slide onto the warm plate.

amarone risotto

Serves 2–3

This pink risotto looks brilliant on a white plate with a light dusting of parmesan, making it a romantic dish for St Valentine's Day. Just add a salad and some good cheese and chocolates to follow. It is much easier to stay home and finish the bottle of wine than to go out and have to take a taxi home.

400 ml (14 fl oz) stock
1 small onion
1 small carrot
1 stick of celery
2 tbsp olive oil
140 g (5 oz) carnaroli rice
200 ml (7 fl oz) Amarone wine
30 g (1 oz) parmesan, grated
20 g (1 oz) butter
salt and pepper

Put the stock in a pot and keep hot. Peel and finely chop the onion, carrot and celery. Heat the oil in a deep, wide frying pan and add the vegetables. Cook over a moderate heat until they are soft.

Add the rice to the pan and coat it well with the fat. Turn the heat up and add a ladle of hot stock. Stir until the stock is absorbed and add the wine, letting it bubble to evaporate the alcohol. Turn down the heat to a moderate simmer – not too slow. Keep stirring. When the rice is just starting to stick, add a ladle of hot stock. Keep stirring. As each ladleful is absorbed, add another. The rice is done when it looks translucent and the chalky bit has gone from the middle.

Start tasting about 10 minutes after the wine goes in. You may not need all the stock. As soon as the rice is done, add the cheese and butter and stir.

roast pumpkin with cumin, thyme and oregano

Serves 4–6

Stored pumpkins make a wonderful alternative to potatoes at this time of year, adding both colour and a change of flavour to meals. Sometimes we cut them in half, remove the seeds and bake them until soft. You can bake squashes and pumpkins with their seeds in, but the strings around the seeds can make the flesh a little watery. Anyway, our gerbil prefers the seeds uncooked. Remove the hot flesh and mash it with orange juice and onions fried until they are brown and crispy. These roast pieces of pumpkin happily look after themselves in a hot oven while you get on with the rest of the meal.

1 pumpkin, about 1 kg (2 lb)

2–3 tbsp olive oil

1 tsp cumin seeds

1 tsp dried thyme

1 tsp dried oregano

salt and pepper

Set the oven to GM6/200°C/400°F.

Cut the pumpkin in half from top to bottom and scoop out the seeds. Cut each half into three wedges and remove the skin. Place the pumpkin wedges on a baking tray. Rub each wedge with oil and sprinkle with cumin seeds, thyme and oregano. Season with salt and pepper. Place in the hot oven for 30 minutes.

potato bread

As the winter wears on, we eat a fair amount of mashed potatoes. If there is leftover mash, we either make potato cakes for frying or add flour and yeast to make a loaf of bread or rolls. The slow proving in the fridge overnight can turn the top grey, but it disappears once the bread is cooked.

The quantities in this recipe are dependent on how much mashed potato is to be used. We use an equal weight of flour to mashed potato and then mix the brown and strong white flours half and half. The volume of water needed depends on how wet the mashed potatoes are. Instead of scones, you can shape the proved dough into a round loaf or two long sausage shapes. Allow about 30–40 minutes to cook.

1 level tsp dried yeast

pinch of sugar

approx. 175 ml (6 fl oz) tepid
    water

330 g (12 oz) mashed potato

165 g (6 oz) strong white flour

165 g (6 oz) fine whole wheat flour

1 tsp salt

Put the yeast in a cup with the pinch of sugar and cover with some of the tepid water. Leave the cup somewhere warm for the yeast to froth up.

Put the mashed potato into a mixing bowl and sift in the flours, adding the bran left in the sieve. Rub the potato through the flours and add the yeast, which should have a head like a pint of stout.

Refill the cup with some of the tepid water and add the salt. Stir until the salt has dissolved and pour into the mixing bowl. Either mix by hand or in a mixer with a dough hook, adding enough water to make a soft dough. Keep kneading until the dough is smooth and springy. Form the dough into a ball and smear it with oil. Cover the bowl and leave it overnight in the fridge to prove.

The next day, take the bowl of dough out of the fridge and let it adjust to room temperature for 45 minutes. Sprinkle a work surface with flour and empty the dough onto the flour. Knead the dough gently, adding enough flour to prevent it from sticking. Gently flatten the dough until it is 2 cm (almost 1 inch) thick. Cut the dough with a 7 cm (3 inch) scone cutter, place the dough circles onto a baking sheet dusted with flour and cover with a tea towel.

Set the oven to GM7/220°C/425°F. Put the baking sheet with the dough circles on top of the cooker while it heats up for 15–20 minutes. When the oven is hot and the scones are rising, place in the oven to bake for 20 minutes. They should be done when browned on top and should sound hollow when turned over and tapped on the bottom.

toasted goat's cheese with winter salad leaves

Serves 4

This frugal salad is a good lunch or starter, and any mix of salad will do. It feels really good to pick the salad leaves just before making it and come back to the warm kitchen knowing that salad does not come any fresher.

1 tbsp sunflower seeds

1 tbsp sesame seeds

1 tbsp pumpkin seeds

8–10 small beetroot leaves

4 handfuls of rocket leaves

12 sorrel leaves

bunch of parsley

4 scallions or 1 large shallot

6 potato bread scones
   (see pp. 42–3) or 12 rounds of
   French baguette, about 1 cm
   (½ inch) thick

Ardsallagh soft goat's cheese or
   Knockalara sheep's cheese

3 tbsp sunflower oil

1 tbsp sesame oil

2–3 tbsp lemon juice

Toast the seeds in a dry pan over a low heat until lightly browned, then remove from the heat to cool.

Wash and dry the salad leaves and parsley and put them in a large bowl with the scallions or shallot.

Split the potato bread scones and toast on one side. Spread the other with goat's cheese. Put the bread and goat's cheese under the grill to heat through and brown.

Dress the salad with the oils and lemon juice and sprinkle with the toasted seeds before tossing. Top with three pieces of goat's cheese on toast and serve.

gremolata-topped fish fillets

Serves 4

Gremolata is the traditional accompaniment sprinkled over osso bucco, consisting of a mixture of lemon zest, garlic and parsley. We had some left over once and we mixed it with breadcrumbs and topped fish fillets with it before baking them in a hot oven. Any white fish will do, such as pollock or whiting, but hake or haddock is better. Adding gremolata to a pot of plain pasta tossed with good olive oil makes a quick meal to remind us of sunnier times.

zest of 1 lemon, unwaxed or
   preferably organic
2 cloves of garlic
large bunch of parsley, chopped
100 g (4 oz) breadcrumbs
lemon juice
salt and pepper
olive oil
4 white fish fillets

Heat the oven to GM6/200°C/400°F.

Remove the zest of the lemon with a grater or zester, leaving the white pith behind. If you use the zester, chop the strips as finely as possible. Finely chop the garlic and mix it with the lemon zest and parsley. Stir the breadcrumbs into the gremolata with a squeeze of lemon juice, a pinch of salt and some pepper.

Oil a roasting tin and lay the fish skin side down. Cover the top of each fillet with a layer of the breadcrumb mix and a dribble of olive oil. Place in the oven for about 20 minutes, more if the fillets are very thick. Serve with wedges of lemon.

loin of bacon with parsley sauce

Serves 6–8

1.5 kg (3 lb) loin of bacon piece
1 stick of celery, chopped
1 carrot, chopped
1 bay leaf
1 small onion, sliced
3 parsley stalks, crushed
4 peppercorns, crushed
brown sugar

Place the bacon in a pot skin side down and cover with water. Bring to the boil on a moderate heat. Skim off any scum that comes to the top and add the celery, carrot, bay leaf, onion, parsley and peppercorns. Put the lid on the pot, turn the heat down to a simmer and cook gently for 1 hour. We pop it in the simmering oven at GM2/150°C/300°F.

Ten minutes before the end of the cooking time, switch the oven on to GM6/200°C/400°F. When the bacon has had a full hour, transfer it to a roasting tray. Score the skin of the bacon and rub it with brown sugar. Put it back in the oven to roast for 20 minutes.

Pour the bacon's cooking liquid through a sieve into a clean pan or jug. It can be used to blanch cabbage or to make soup, but do taste for saltiness. When the bacon is done, put it on a serving plate and carve. Serve with parsley sauce.

Parsley sauce

570 ml (1 pint) milk
2 bunches of parsley
60 g (2 oz) butter
60 g (2 oz) plain flour
salt and pepper

Pour the milk into a saucepan and place on a low heat. Take the leaves off the parsley and set aside. Take the stalks of the parsley and twist them over the pan of milk, so that they are crushed, then add them to the milk with a pinch of salt. Bring the milk to the boil, then take off the heat and leave to infuse for 10 minutes.

Finely chop the leaves of parsley. Melt the butter in a pot, add the flour and stir. Cook until it is a light gold colour. Take the pot off the heat and add some of the milk through a sieve. Stir well, as it will be quite thick. Add more milk through the sieve, and stir well again. Keep adding a little milk and stirring until all the milk is added.

Put the pot back on a moderate heat and add the chopped parsley leaves. Stir constantly until the sauce comes to the boil and thickens. Turn the heat down and simmer for 2 minutes, stirring often so as not to let the bottom burn. Pour into a sauce boat or jug to serve.

pancakes

Makes about 12

Pancakes with butter, sugar and lemon, applied in that order while the pancake is still on the pan, then rolled or folded over to be eaten immediately are just...yummy! Not an everyday healthy dish, but a must once a year on Shrove Tuesday.

And yes, we do fill them with savoury stuffings, such as ham and grated cheese, chicken and leek pie filling or the end of the loin of bacon chopped into some parsley sauce (see pp. 48–9). We also experiment with different flours, adding half fine whole wheat or buckwheat flour. These give the pancakes more flavour and are tastier with the savoury fillings.

110 g (4 oz) plain flour
pinch of salt
1 egg
300 ml (10 fl oz) milk
oil

Sift the flour into a bowl and add the salt. Stir with a whisk. Break the egg and add to the flour and salt. Gently mix the egg into some of the flour to form a paste. As the flour and egg thicken, add the milk a splash at a time, and incorporate more and more flour and milk until all the milk is used and the batter looks like thin cream. Pour the batter into a jug. If the batter is lumpy, pour it through a sieve.

Have butter, sugar and lemon ready by the side of the hob, as once you start, there's no stopping until all the batter is used (at least in our house!).

Heat a frying pan on a medium heat and rub the pan with kitchen paper dipped in oil. (Use a wooden clothes peg to hold the paper and you won't burn your fingers.)

Pour some of the batter into the pan and tilt it so that the pan is completely covered in batter. When the batter looks dry on top and begins to brown at the edges, slide a fish slice underneath and turn the pancake over. Smear with a little butter, sprinkle with sugar and a squeeze of lemon juice. Roll or fold the pancake over and serve straight from the pan.

march

garden

If you believe the gardening books, March is one of the busiest months in the calendar, but you have to remember that most of these tomes refer to conditions in the south of England. Irish gardeners often find that our gardening seasons can lag a fortnight or even a month behind what happens in Surrey.

Nevertheless, there is a lot to be done, especially if you have a greenhouse or polytunnel, in which crops can be started under protection and planted out when the spring has really sprung.

It's easier, perhaps, to list the vegetables that can't be transplanted than those that can. Don't attempt transplanting with carrots, parsnips, beetroots, turnips or, indeed, any root crop. You can get an extra early crop of beetroot by sowing in biodegradable pots that are eventually planted straight into the soil outside, but even with this minimal disturbance you'll end up with a few very strangely formed roots.

The kitchen windowsill is crowded during March, thronged with the tender plants that can't be entrusted to the chilly protection of the polytunnel. There are tomatoes, peppers, aubergines and cucumbers, and we usually have a few courgettes under cover for an early crop.

The trick here is to choose one of the new F^1 hybrid varieties that produce only fruit-bearing female flowers. Normal courgettes will produce lots of male flowers until the temperature rises enough to make the females feel comfortable, and only then do you get courgettes. The F^1 all-female variety called Partenon fruits by mid-May in the polytunnel, at a time when we would hesitate to sow a normal variety out of doors. To be honest, we are usually sick of courgettes by midsummer.

March is when our thoughts turn to brassicas, the great cabbage family that is the repository of so many so-called superfoods. Normal gardeners sow cabbages, broccoli, Brussels sprouts, cauliflowers and what have you in the open ground and thin the plants until they are the desired distance apart. We don't because we think it's an awful waste. Instead, we sow brassicas in pots or modules in the polytunnel, three seeds to each. The seedlings are then thinned to the strongest one, and we end up a month later with terrific little plants that are ready to be planted out at the ideal spacing and in balmier conditions.

In March, the polytunnel is a mass of pots and modules sown not just with brassicas, but also with lettuce, chard, spinach and French beans (the last being intended for planting out in the polytunnel because only the best Irish summers seem to suit them). This is also the time for sowing the first of two batches of parsley (the second lot will be done in August to keep us going through the winter).

There is a certain snobbery about parsley. The flat-leaf sort is very much in fashion, while the curly version, with which we all grew up, is looked upon as being a bit naff. We prefer flat-leaf or Continental parsley for salads, but for other purposes the curly stuff is just fine.

Parsley can take a very long time to germinate. Despair is indicated when more than three months have passed, but we find that most of our sowings come up within a few weeks. Basil and coriander, which are also sown now, come up like lightning in comparison.

Outside, the picture is less busy. By mid-March a few sowings will have been made: turnip (not swede), radishes, parsnips, scallions and peas. The radishes and the parsnips will have been sown together: the parsnips are sown four seeds every foot or so with the radishes in between. This is because parsnips can take several weeks to come up, while radishes jump from the ground within days and they mark the row. The parsnips are eventually thinned to one plant at each station.

We plant our early spuds on St Patrick's Day, or at least by the weekend after, because it's good to have a deadline, and also because it's an old Irish tradition. This tends to be a family affair, as it's quite an onerous task. Trenches are dug the width of a spade and a generous six inches deep, and well-rotted manure is barrowed up to the vegetable garden and dumped in.

Each seed potato is then examined, and all but the two or three strongest shoots are rubbed off. They are then pushed into the bed of manure, which is about three inches deep, and each one is given a large scoop of wood ash, which we have been saving from the stoves all winter. This provides potash (and, so they say, some protection from subterranean slugs) while the manure provides nitrogen. All organic!

Each little tuber with its delicate shoots is then gently covered with earth before the trench is filled in – but not firmed – leaving a ridge that stands about three inches proud of the surrounding earth.

Doubtless it all sounds very wholesome and jolly, but if, like us, your minimum spud planting consists of four rows, each thirty feet long, it's a hard day's work. And that's before the rows of main crops that will be planted in April.

Our poor Jerusalem artichokes often get short shrift, usually because we forget to plant them until the spuds are in. And because they are planted in exactly the same way, except for being placed a foot and a half apart and having the soil gently firmed, it all seems like more of the same. But come November, we are glad of them, even if their planting has been rather unceremonious. They are quite forgiving. And quite delicious.

recipes

March is preparation time in earnest in the garden. Any sunny days and signs of spring, such as primroses and daffodils, are gladly welcomed. Our food is still of the comfort variety – soups and stews with sprouting broccoli or other greens or leeks from the garden.

artichoke soup with rosemary

Serves 4

This soup is a variation on the stoved artichokes (p. 66). They are cooked in the same way except with stock added and puréed. If we think ahead, we can cook extra artichokes to have soup the next day.

2 tbsp lemon juice or vinegar

15 Jerusalem artichokes

3 cloves of garlic

1 onion

3 tbsp olive oil

2 sprigs of rosemary

850 ml (1½ pints) chicken stock or water

salt and pepper

Pour the lemon juice or vinegar into a big bowl of water. Quickly peel the artichokes and add to the water and lemon juice to prevent them from turning grey. Gently crush the garlic with the flat of a knife and remove the skin. Peel and slice the onion.

Pour the oil into a wide pot and put it on a medium heat. Add the garlic, onion, rosemary and artichokes. When the contents of the pot start to sizzle, cover with a lid and turn the heat to low. Let them cook away slowly in their own steam, shaking the pot and stirring every 5 minutes or so. If during this time the onion starts to get too dark, add some of the water or stock; you need to let the vegetables colour a little, but not burn.

When the vegetables begin to soften, add half the water or stock and bring to the boil and simmer for 15 minutes, until the artichokes are soft. Let the soup cool a little, or add some more of the water or stock. Fish out the rosemary sprigs and purée the contents of the pot.

Return the purée to a clean pot and taste, seasoning as necessary. Thin the soup with the rest of the water or stock, bring back to the boil and simmer for 3–4 minutes. Serve.

caldo verde

Serves 4

This Portuguese soup is a first cousin of coddle, but the potatoes are mashed to a rough purée and then the greens and chorizo are added. This is a meal in itself with a salad and some bread.

1 kg (2 lb) floury potatoes

1.45 litres (2.5 pints) stock

2 cloves of garlic, skinned and chopped

3 small chorizo sausages, about 260 g (9 oz) total

460 g (1 lb) cabbage or kale

salt and pepper

Peel the potatoes and cut into small chunks. Heat the stock in a large pot and add the potatoes and garlic. Bring to the boil and simmer until the potatoes are soft, about 15–20 minutes.

Cut the chorizo into 1 cm ($\frac{1}{2}$ inch) slices and shred the kale into narrow ribbons, removing the tough stalks.

When the potatoes are soft, crush them in the stock with a potato masher or the back of a wooden spoon, to a rough purée. Add the chorizo slices and the kale to the pot; bring back to the boil and simmer for 5–10 minutes. Taste, add salt and pepper if necessary, and serve.

potatoes dauphinoise

Serves 4

This is comfort food, pure and simple. We like this with lamb, a roast or plain grilled chops. It is best made with soapy potatoes, but Roosters will do at this time of year.

60 g (2 oz) butter
800 g (1 lb 12 oz) potatoes
2 cloves of garlic
pepper
nutmeg
250 ml (10 fl oz) cream

Butter an ovenproof dish and set the oven to GM5/190°C/375°F.

Wash the potatoes and peel if their skins aren't great. Slice into thin slices about 3 mm ($1/10$ inch) thick. Peel and thinly slice the garlic.

Sprinkle the buttered dish with a quarter of the garlic, some freshly ground pepper and grated nutmeg. Lay a quarter of the potatoes in an even layer into the dish. Sprinkle with another third of the garlic, pepper and nutmeg. Continue with the layers, ending with a layer of potato.

Pour over the cream and add the rest of the butter, some more pepper and nutmeg. Cover the dish with a butter paper or greaseproof paper and bake for 30 minutes. Take the paper off and cook for another 15 minutes to brown the top.

champ

Serves 4–6

More comfort food, and with potatoes coming to the end of their stored season, this is a good way to use them up.

1 kg (2 lb) potatoes
250 ml (8 fl oz) milk
80 g (3 oz) butter
8 scallions, chopped
salt and pepper

Wash and peel the potatoes. Steam until soft. Scald the milk while you mash the potatoes with the butter. Beat in the hot milk and chopped scallions to the mashed potatoes. Taste and season with salt and pepper.

pumpkin and feta quiche

Serves 4–6

Some varieties of pumpkin will store until March if they are kept cool and dry.

Pastry

60 g (2 oz) fine wholemeal flour

170 g (6 oz) plain flour

110 g (4 oz) cold butter

80 ml (3 fl oz) cold water (more or less may be needed depending on the flour)

Set the oven to GM6/200°C/400°F.

Put the flours into a food processor and whiz for a moment. Cut the butter into cubes and add to the flours. Whiz for about 10–15 seconds to rub the butter into the flour. With the motor still running, add the water. Keep mixing until the pastry forms a ball. Wrap the pastry and leave to rest for 15 minutes.

Roll out the pastry and line a 21 cm (8 inch) loose-bottomed tin. Cover the pastry with greaseproof paper and some baking beans and bake for 15 minutes.

Filling

100 g (4 oz) of 2 cm (¾ inch) cubes of pumpkin flesh

1 small onion, peeled and sliced

150 g (5 oz) of 2 cm (¾ inch) cubes of feta or Knockalara cheese

2 eggs

enough cream to make 300 ml (10 fl oz), including the eggs

salt and pepper

Heat the oven to GM6/200°C/400°F.

Spread the pumpkin over the bottom of the pastry case and sprinkle with the onion and cheese. Crack the eggs into a measuring jug and add enough cream to reach the 300 ml (10 fl oz) mark. Add a pinch of salt and beat the eggs and cream with a fork. Pour it over the pumpkin mix and sprinkle with some pepper.

Bake in the oven for 30 minutes, until the top is browned and the centre just set.

purple sprouting broccoli and hollandaise

Serves 4

The flavour of purple sprouting broccoli (PSB) is like refined cabbage, but not cabbagey. We put it on a par with asparagus as a seasonal treat. It's mainly only available to home gardeners, as it rarely makes it to supermarkets. Country markets and farmers' markets do get it, but the season is short.

We share the first small picks of PSB as a starter with melted butter or some hollandaise. As it gets more abundant, we use it in quiche or as a vegetable with a main course. We find steaming is the best method of cooking PSB, as it doesn't make it overly wet and it's easier to test for doneness.

To prepare the PSB, trim into even lengths and place in a steamer basket. Bring 5 cm (2 inches) of water to the boil in the bottom of the steamer. Put the steamer basket on top with the lid on and steam for 3–5 minutes. Test with a fork that the stems are tender and remove from the steamer when done. Pat the PSB with kitchen paper to remove excess moisture. Divide the PSB onto warm plates and spoon over a little melted butter or hollandaise sauce.

tom's hollandaise

50 g (2 oz) salted butter

100 g (4 oz) unsalted butter

1 shallot

2 tbsp water

1 tbsp white wine vinegar

1 large egg yolk

Cut the butters into 2 cm ($^3/_4$ inch) cubes and allow them to warm up to room temperature. Peel and slice the shallot. Pour the water and vinegar into a small saucepan and add the shallot. Put the pot on to boil. Boil the liquid until it's reduced to only one dessertspoonful. Remove from the heat and strain the reduced liquid into the top of a double boiler and discard the shallot.

Put 5 cm (2 inches) of very hot water into the bottom of the double boiler and place on a very low heat. The water in the bottom of the double boiler should be hot, but not boiling, so that the steam heats the top. Add the egg yolk to the vinegar and whisk them together for a moment before putting the top onto the double boiler. Whisk until the egg starts to thicken, then add the butter a cube at a time, until all the butter is added and the sauce is thick.

If it gets too hot and starts to crack, take the top off the double boiler and whisk in 4 or 5 cubes of butter in one go to cool it down. If you want to be extra safe, have a bowl of really cold water in the sink that you can cool the top of the double boiler.

Using 4 to 6 stalks of purple sprouting broccoli per person, trim the PSB, place in a steamer basket and steam over boiling water for about 3–4 minutes. The stems should give to a fork and the tops should be bright green. Place on kitchen paper to dry for a moment and then onto hot plates. Pour over some hollandaise sauce and serve.

stoved artichokes

Jerusalem artichokes have a delicate flavour similar to their very distant globe artichoke cousins. Jerusalem artichokes are knobbly roots that have a stormy effect on the lower gut. We nicknamed them, not very politely, 'fartichokes'. They contain inulin, a prebiotic that feeds gut flora and helps balance blood sugar.

When peeled, they discolour quite quickly. If you want to keep them as white as possible, put 2 tablespoons of lemon juice or vinegar into a bowl of water and put them into it as you peel. Once they are cooked and browned, they're fine.

Per person

1 tbsp olive oil

3–4 artichokes, peeled

2 small shallots, peeled

1 clove of garlic, peeled and bruised

1 sprig of rosemary about 6 cm (2 inches) long

1 sprig of thyme

½ bay leaf

salt and pepper

1 tbsp water

Put the oil into a heavy-based frying pan at a medium heat. When the oil has heated, add the artichokes, shallots and garlic. Stir and coat with oil and sprinkle the herbs on top. Sprinkle with salt and pepper and add the water.

Put the lid on the pan and turn up the heat. When you hear sizzling, shake the pan. Do this 3 or 4 times and then turn the heat to low or place in the oven. Cook on a gentle heat, occasionally shaking the pan until the artichokes and shallots are tender, about 15–20 minutes. Watch that they don't get too dry and start to burn. Add some more water to the pan if necessary.

Take the lid off and turn up the heat, boil off the remaining moisture and let the artichokes and shallots brown in places.

ray/skate with black butter

Serves 4

When we eat fish, we tend to do nothing more than dust it with flour, fry it in a little oil and serve it with some vegetables or a salad. Ray – or skate, as it is sometimes called – is a wonderful flat fish with a very rough skin that is hard to remove. Some fish shops will take the skin off for you, but if they don't, the skin will peel off easily after poaching it. Ray is a good fish for people who don't like fish bones, because it has a layer of cartilage instead of fine bones. The cooked flesh is easily scraped from the layer of cartilage.

1 kg (2 lb) ray/skate in 4 pieces
water
1 shallot, peeled and sliced
3 peppercorns
2 cm (¾ inch) piece of carrot, peeled and chopped
1 small stick of celery, chopped
½ tsp salt
1 lemon
80 g (3 oz) butter
3 tbsp parsley, chopped
1 tbsp capers, drained and rinsed

Put the plates into the oven to warm up.

Wipe the pieces of ray and lay them in a single layer in a pan and cover with cold water. Add the shallot, peppercorns, carrot, celery and salt. Cut the lemon in half and squeeze one half, then add 1 tablespoon of the lemon juice to the pan with the fish.

Bring the pan to the boil and then to a simmer. Simmer the fish until the flesh can be easily pulled from the bones; this takes about 15 minutes. Take the pan off the heat and remove the skin from the pieces of ray if necessary. Keep the ray warm.

In a heavy frying pan, melt the butter and let it go brown, then add the parsley, capers and the rest of the lemon juice. Let it bubble for a minute and then remove from the heat.

Drain the pieces of ray and place them on the warm plates. Share out the black butter between them. Cut the other lemon half into four wedges and serve with the ray.

coddle

Serves 4–6

People either love or hate coddle. The look of it isn't very appealing – pink sausages and rasher pieces floating in a soup of crumbling potato chunks, flecked with parsley and onion. We make it with the meatiest sausages, homemade chicken stock and lots of parsley just before serving. It is particularly good on a cold, wet day with a baked apple or fruit crumble to follow.

2 onions or leeks
200 g (7 oz) streaky rasher piece
850 ml (1½ pints) stock
8 good sausages
8–10 potatoes
big bunch of parsley
salt and pepper

Peel and thinly slice the onions or leeks. Cut the streaky rasher piece into approx. 3 cm (1 inch) cubes. Put the stock into a large pot and add the onions, rasher pieces and sausages. Bring the contents of the pot slowly to the boil.

Wash the potatoes and if the skins look good, leave them unpeeled. Cut the potatoes into chunks that will fit one to a soup spoon and add them to the pot.

Top up the pot with water so that everything is just submerged. Bring to the boil, then reduce to a simmer until the potatoes break apart when poked with a knife; try not to let them disintegrate.

While the coddle is cooking, wash and finely chop the parsley. Taste the coddle and season with salt and pepper. Add the chopped parsley to the pot and gently stir through. Serve in soup bowls with a knife, fork and spoon.

april

garden

April sees the kitchen windowsill gradually return to normal as its occupants are planted outside. The three or four courgette plants are planted four feet apart, as they can become monsters in time, and on top of little mounds in the polytunnel, below each of which lies a couple of buckets of manure or compost. At nighttime they are cosseted with a blanket of bubble wrap until the danger of a heavy frost has passed.

The more delicate cucumbers will be given similar treatment towards the end of the month. The tomatoes are planted in rows three to four feet apart and the aubergines, which will grow into sturdy little bushes, go in between. The soil will have had a good feed of organic matter before planting and later, when they are about to set fruit in late May, there will be a weekly dose of wood ash.

By the time all of this has been done, the windowsill will have received two new residents: a tray of celery and a tray of celeriac. It's curious that these relatively tough and closely related plants (they survive fairly happily in the ground well into winter) are so tender when they are very young.

Both are sown broadcast, scattered very thinly on moist compost in seed trays. The celeriac seeds are then covered with a gossamer sprinkling of compost and firmed down, but the celery seeds aren't covered at all because they need light to germinate. When the minute seedlings are just starting to produce the first true leaves, they are excavated very, very gently and transplanted into modules or pots. This is a very delicate business and, to be honest, I'm not sure that the stringy, coarse celery that we have so far managed to grow is really worth the trouble.

On the other hand, celeriac is a pure joy and one of those vegetables which really cheers up the dark days of winter. Once the delicate stage is over and the seedlings have grown up a bit in the polytunnel, they can be planted out in early summer into ground which has as much organic matter in it as you can possibly manage. This is critical for both celery and celeriac, as is an abundance of water.

The most important task for us at the dawn of April lies outdoors. This is the simple matter of sowing leeks, without which so much of the year would be very drab indeed. We select two or sometimes three varieties which will crop from early autumn right through to late spring, as we want what the old gardeners used to call succession. They are sown, quite thickly, in rows a foot apart where they will grow happily until they are about a foot high, some of them as thick as a pencil. Then it will be time to plant them out into permanent positions where they will swell to full size.

At the same time, we generally put in a row or two of carrots which, with a bit of luck, will have reached a reasonable size before the dreaded carrot fly strikes, as it always does, around midsummer. They can be sown quite close together as they aren't intended to become big, full-grown roots, but the rows need to be a foot or more apart.

If the weather has been kind and we aren't too busy, we usually plant onion sets by the end of March, but very often this task – and it is quite a task – is deferred until early April. I think it may have something to do with the spud-planting. Shallots tend to go in before the onions, simply because it's an easier job. You simply push the base of each shallot into some firm earth and leave most of it showing above ground. Spaced eight inches apart, each shallot will have divided into half a dozen or so new ones by the end of July. This is the easiest vegetable of all, essentially a small and very mild onion.

We like to plant between 400 and 500 onion sets, four inches apart, with six inches between the rows. That's enough space to allow these little bulblets to develop into the kind of onions that are neither too big nor too fiddly to use in the kitchen. We feed the onion plot with a few barrow loads of old manure and scatter some seaweed fertilizer in for good measure, but it's important to avoid giving too much nitrogen, as this can make the onions too soft for storing over the winter.

Planting onions couldn't be simpler, although it's quite monotonous if you grow as many as we do. You simply push each little bulb firmly into the ground until only the very tip is showing. After a couple of days, you may need to replant those that have been pulled up by inquisitive birds (some of whom are so dense that they can uproot a whole row before they twig that it won't get any more exciting).

By the end of April, the first shoots of the new potatoes should have pushed through and there is still a danger that they may get scorched by a late frost. It's not the end of the world if this happens, but it's better to avoid such a check to growth. Simply draw some soil over the emerging leaves with a hoe or a spade every evening. Apart from anything else, this exercise will reassure you that the spuds are indeed growing.

Rhubarb is one of the easiest things we grow. In fact, it grows itself. We inherited an old rhubarb patch which requires only a top dressing of compost or manure in the late autumn to produce an abundance of bright stalks by spring.

recipes

April is when spring starts to take off, with loads of spring flowers, but it can still be cold. The first rhubarb to stew gently or make into a crumble arrives in April. Just as mince pies are part of Christmas, so hot cross buns are part of Easter, perhaps more so than Easter eggs, which seem to arrive in the shops before Lent even starts.

The leeks have to be used up as the ground is needed for other crops. Stored potatoes are coming to the end of their best, starting to sprout and wanting to grow, and the pumpkins and squashes are gone.

nettle soup

Serves 4

Brotchán neanntóg. As this is the Hungry Gap, it's good to use what is naturally available. Try to serve this as soon as it's ready, otherwise the colour loses its vibrancy.

2 tbsp oil

60 g (2 oz) oatmeal

2 leeks

bowl of nettle tops, about
   110 g (4 oz)

1 litre (1¾ pints) water or stock

salt, pepper and nutmeg

300 ml (10 fl oz) milk

2 tbsp parsley, chopped

If you only have rolled oats, chop them in a food processor for 15–20 seconds.

Heat the oil in a pot and add the oatmeal. Cook until it's turning golden and add the stock or water.

Clean and chop the leeks. While wearing rubber gloves, wash the nettles and chop them. The food processor is very good for chopping them.

Add the leeks and the chopped nettles to the stock and oatmeal. Bring to the boil, season with salt and pepper and a grating or two of nutmeg and simmer for 30 minutes. Taste and adjust the seasoning. Add the milk and the parsley. Bring to the boil and serve.

leeks wrapped in prosciutto

Serves 4 as a main course or 6 as a side dish

The size of the leeks is all-important in this recipe; they must be of even diameter. If you
have a mix of thick and thin leeks, the thicker ones may be sliced in half lengthways after
steaming.

12 thin leeks

45 g (1 1/2 oz) butter

45 g (1 1/2 oz) brown flour

450 ml (15 fl oz) milk

150 g (5 oz) strong white cheddar, grated

6 slices of prosciutto

1 large egg

Put some water into the bottom of a steamer to heat. Clean the leeks and cut into similar lengths. Place into the steamer for 5–8 minutes. They should be hot all the way through and starting to cook.

Set the oven to GM6/200°C/400°F and begin making the cheese sauce by heating the butter and flour in a saucepan over a moderate heat. When the mixture begins to sizzle, start stirring and cook for a further couple of minutes without burning.

Take the pan off the heat and add a little of the milk, whisking it well into the flour and butter. Keep adding and whisking the milk into the mixture until all the milk is added and the sauce is smooth.

Return the pan to the heat and bring the sauce to the boil, whisking all the time. When the sauce starts to boil, turn down the heat to low and let it simmer for about 3 minutes, whisking often to stop it burning. Add 100 g (4 oz) of the grated cheese to the sauce and take it off the heat.

Butter an ovenproof dish that will hold the leeks in a single layer. Cut each slice of prosciutto in half lengthways and wrap each half slice around a leek and place in the dish.

Whisk the egg into the cheese sauce and pour it over the top of the leeks. Sprinkle the rest of the cheese over the sauce and bake in the hot oven for 25 minutes.

amy's cheesy leek bake

Serves 4–6

Amy is one of our eldest daughter's, Sarah's, friends and we were treated to this one night at her house when we were there for dinner. Amy was given the recipe as part of her home economics classes in school; it seems that traditional cookery is still alive in Irish schools.

3 medium–large leeks
butter
salt and pepper
2 eggs
200 ml (7 fl oz) cream
85 g (3 oz) cheese, grated

Set the oven to GM5/190°C/375°F.

Clean and slice the leeks into 2 cm ($^3/_4$ inch) rounds. Put a knob of butter into a frying pan and place on a moderate heat. When the butter has melted, add the leeks and cook until they begin to soften.

Butter an ovenproof dish and put the leeks into it. Season with salt and pepper. Whisk the eggs and cream together and pour over the leeks. Sprinkle the top with grated cheese and bake in the oven until browned and bubbling, about 30–40 minutes.

chicken and leek pie

Serves 4–6

We are really lucky to live in an area that has an organic egg and chicken producer. We tend to buy whole chickens fresh, joint them ourselves and freeze the pieces we don't use straight away. When it comes to clearing out the freezer, this is how we use up the assortment of pieces.

6 chicken pieces
100 ml (4 fl oz) white wine
1 carrot, chopped
1 stick of celery, chopped
handful of leek greens, chopped
1 bay leaf
salt and pepper
6 leeks
20 g (1 oz) butter
1 tsp arrowroot or corn flour
100 ml (4 fl oz) cream

Put the chicken pieces into a pot. Add the wine and enough water to cover the chicken. Bring to the boil and skim off any scum that comes to the surface. Add the carrot, celery, leek greens, bay leaf and seasoning. Bring the pot back to the boil and let it simmer for about 30 minutes (by then, the chicken should be tender and cooked through).

While the chicken is cooking, wash and slice the leeks into 1 cm ($^1/_2$ inch) pieces. Melt the butter in a frying pan and soften the leeks over a moderate heat.

Take the chicken pieces out of the pot. Put the pot on a high heat and as you skin and bone the chicken pieces, put the skin and bones back into the pot with the cooking broth. Keep the meat warm in the pie dish with a ladleful of the strained broth. Add the leeks to the chicken meat. Take the pot off the heat and strain off the broth.

Slake the arrowroot or corn flour in a little cold water and add some hot broth. Pour this into a small saucepan and bring to the boil. Add the cream and heat through, then pour over the chicken and leeks. Top the pie with rolled out pastry and bake in a hot oven until the pastry is browned.

Flaky pastry

250 g (9 oz) plain flour

185 g (6 oz) very cold butter

150–160 ml (5 fl oz) cold water

Sift the flour into a bowl, cut the butter into small cubes about 1 cm ($\frac{1}{2}$ inch) square and gently stir into the flour. Pour in the cold water and mix to a stiff dough with a knife. Shape into a rough rectangle, wrap and leave to cool in the fridge for 30 minutes.

Remove from the fridge and place on a floured surface. Roll out into a 1 cm ($\frac{1}{2}$ inch) thick rectangle with a floured rolling pin. Fold the pastry in three and turn so that the three layers are towards you, roll out again, fold in three again, turn, roll and fold again. Wrap and leave in the fridge for 1 hour.

lamb hot pot

Serves 6 or one very hungry Roberta

Arriving home on a dark, wet evening, it's wonderful to take this out of the bottom oven and finish it in the roasting oven while the riding kit is put away and the hands washed. A dish of guacamole and carrot sticks adds to the veg count and helps to assuage the hunger pangs while it browns.

oil

6–8 lamb gigot chops, depending on size (and appetites)

salt and pepper

2 onions

4 sprigs of thyme

3 medium carrots

6–8 potatoes, not too floury

300 ml (10 fl oz) boiling stock or water

Set the oven to GM3/170°C/340°F. Heat some oil in a frying pan and brown the chops on both sides. Place in a large ovenproof dish and season with salt and pepper.

Peel and slice the onions and soften in the pan with a little extra oil. When the onions are soft, spread them over the chops and add the sprigs of thyme. Peel and slice the carrots into $\frac{1}{2}$ cm ($\frac{1}{4}$ inch) thick slices and spread in a single layer over the chops. If the skins on the potatoes are good, just scrub them; if not, peel them, then slice them into 1 cm ($\frac{1}{2}$ inch) thick slices. Layer the sliced potatoes over the top.

Pour on the stock or water and cover the top of the dish with a lid or oiled greaseproof paper. Bake at the centre of the oven for 90 minutes, then remove the lid or paper and increase the heat to GM4/180°C/350°F for 30 minutes to brown the top.

rhubarb crumble

Serves 6

Oats were the original staple grain in Ireland and this oaty topping is a tribute to that. As the measurements are all in spoonfuls, you don't even need the weighing scales.

bunch of rhubarb, or 6–7 sticks

sugar to taste

2 tbsp water

6 tbsp rolled oats

3 tbsp brown flour

3 tbsp brown sugar

1 tbsp hazelnuts, chopped

3 tbsp sunflower oil

Set the oven to GM5/190°C/375°F. Cut the rhubarb into 2 cm (³/₄ inch) pieces and put into a 20 cm x 25 cm (8 inch x 10 inch) ovenproof dish. Sprinkle with sugar and the water.

Mix together the oats, flour, sugar, nuts and oil in a bowl and spread over the top of the rhubarb. Bake in the oven for 20–30 minutes. Serve with cool whipped cream or custard.

hot cross buns

Makes 12 buns

By growing our own vegetables, we have become more aware of the changing seasons and this gives us an insight into how the ancient and religious festivals were a way of marking the passing of the seasons. By Good Friday, when these enriched bread rolls were traditionally served, the worst of the winter was over and spring had started. They are also a good way of using up the dried fruit left over from Christmas.

1 tsp dried yeast or 20 g (1 oz)
   fresh yeast or 1 sachet of
   fast-action yeast

300 ml (10 fl oz) hand-hot milk

450 g (1 lb) strong white flour

85 g (3 oz) sugar

1 level tsp salt

2 tsp mixed spice

170 g (6 oz) mixed dried fruit

85 g (3 oz) soft butter, cubed

1 dessertspoon oil

2 tbsp sugar

2 tbsp milk

The temperature of the milk is correct when you can hold your little finger in it and count to 10 and it feels the same as your finger, neither too hot nor too cold.

Mix the dried or fresh yeast with a tablespoonful of the milk and a good pinch of the sugar and leave to froth, about 10–15 minutes depending on the temperature.

Sift the flour into a bowl and sprinkle in the rest of the sugar, salt, spice, dried fruit, the sachet of fast-action yeast if you are using it and the cubed butter. Gently mix the contents of the bowl and make a well in the centre. Pour in the frothing yeast and the warm milk. Mix well to make a soft dough.

Knead the dough in a mixer with a dough hook or by hand on a floured surface until it is smooth and springy. Shape the dough into a ball and smear it with the oil, then leave to rise in a bowl covered with a plastic bag or a damp cloth.

When the dough has doubled in size, about 90 minutes to 3 hours depending on temperature, turn the dough out on a floured surface and divide into 12 pieces. Shape into round balls and place on a baking tray dusted with flour. Cover with a clean tea towel and leave somewhere warm to rise for 30–40 minutes.

After 20–25 minutes, set the oven to GM6/200°C/400°F and uncover the buns. Mark a cross on each bun with a knife and cover them up again until the oven has reached its temperature. Bake the buns for 15–20 minutes, until brown and hollow when tapped underneath.

Boil the sugar and the milk until syrupy and brush over the buns while still hot, allowing for two coats. This gives the buns a nice shine. Cool the buns on a wire rack and eat the same day.

rhubarb and ginger jam

Makes about 5–6 pots of jam

The first few pots of this jam are always lapped up, but as soon as there is strawberry jam or raspberry jam on offer, it gets pushed to the back of the larder until they are all gone.

1 kg (2 lb) rhubarb
3 cm (1 inch) length of fresh ginger
1 kg (2 lb) sugar
juice of 2 lemons
6 glass jars and jam pot covers

For hints and tips on jam making, see Seville Orange Marmalade, pp. 26–7.

Cut the rhubarb into 2 cm (³/₄ inch) pieces. Grate or finely chop the ginger and mix with the rhubarb and sugar in a ceramic or glass bowl. Pour in the lemon juice and leave overnight.

Transfer to a steel or enamelled saucepan and slowly bring to the boil, stirring well to dissolve the sugar before it boils. Put the jars into the oven at GM1/140°C/285°F.

Boil the jam fast until the setting point is reached, usually about 15–20 minutes (see pp. 26–7).

Take the pot off the heat and let it cool for about 10 minutes. Ladle into the hot jam pots. Cover with the waxed discs smooth side down, followed by the cellophane discs dampened and held in place with the rubber bands.

crystallised primroses

This is a lovely thing to do with these pretty flowers to use as decoration on a cake. Our daughter Georgia revived this ancient tradition for us. Please do not pick primroses from the wild. We are lucky to have them growing on our land, but even so, we would only pick as many as we need. Wildflower seeds to grow your own are available. Later in the year, rose petals may be used in the same way.

Collect clean, dry primrose flowers on a bright day. Lightly whisk an egg white and, using a paintbrush, paint each of the flowers with some egg white and then dust them with caster sugar. Leave them to dry on a sheet of baking parchment somewhere warm. We put them on a cooling rack and leave it on the lid of the Aga's simmering plate or in the hot press.

may

garden

The first job for us in May, and it's a pleasant one, is tying the tomato plants to stakes or bamboos. There's something very enticing about the green, pungent smell of tomato foliage on a warm day in early summer. Now is the time when we must start taking out the side shoots too. Unless the tomato is a bush variety, which you simply let grow and grow, side shoots have to be removed in order to encourage fruiting and a manageable shape.

This is easier than it sounds. The stem of a non-bush tomato plant has leaves every few inches and in the joint between the leaf and the stem, shoots grow. Simply pinch them out. You will need to check at least once a week and take action accordingly. They say that when five or six trusses of fruit have set, you should pinch out the main growing tip of the plant so as to concentrate its energy on fruit ripening, but I have to say we have never found that it makes much difference.

If you are very thrifty, you may like to take some of the side shoots which you have carefully removed, dip them in hormone-rooting powder and plant them in moist compost. In a couple of weeks they will have become independent tomato plants.

Picking your sweetcorn and plunging it, within minutes, into boiling water is one of those experiences that underline, even for the most cynical, the value of growing your own. But in order to do so, you must think ahead.

Around the middle of May, we sow our sweetcorn in modules in the polytunnel: one of the large seeds to each module, covered with a half inch of compost. The speed with which it germinates always takes us by surprise; I think the record is five days. The seedlings look like scutch or couch grass at first and they grow very rapidly.

They can be planted outside in early June or under cover pretty much straight away. We tend to take the latter route, as we are blessed with plenty of space in the

polytunnel. If the seedlings are bound for the great outdoors, we're careful to place the modules on a solid surface and not on the ground. This is because the roots will delve through the modules and into the soil; they won't enjoy the disturbance when they are yanked up for transplanting.

Sweetcorn, whether grown inside or out, is best planted equidistantly on a grid pattern. As little as a foot apart each way will work, especially as such close planting facilitates pollination. Sweetcorn pollen is produced at the top of the plant and it then falls onto the silky, sticky tassels that protrude from the nascent cobs that grow lower down. Under cover, it's a good idea to give the plants a shake every day or so in order to help this process.

The same goes for tomatoes, or so they say. Often the first flowers will have opened before the end of May, although the pollen has a tiny journey to make by comparison to that of sweetcorn. Tomatoes are said to appreciate assistance. Tapping the stem or spraying the plant with a mist of water, at around noon, will aid pollination.

By the end of May, it's safe to sow courgettes and marrows outdoors. The best way to do this is to prepare however many planting stations you need by digging holes, filling them with plenty of manure and piling the soil back in so as to make a series of mounds. Sow a single seed an inch deep on each mound and cover with a mini-cloche, made by cutting a large, clear plastic bottle in two. This will help to warm the soil and to protect the seedling when it pushes through.

We only occasionally grow courgettes outside and prefer to use exactly the same growing technique to produce their much more interesting cousins, the squashes. The only difference is that while most courgettes grow on bushy plants, the squashes produce long shoots which trail all over the place. This doesn't bother us as we have lots of space, but in a small garden it could be a headache. On the other hand, squashes can be trained up fences and over outbuildings. And they are most certainly worth it.

Our favourites are the orange-fleshed mini-pumpkin called Baby Bear which weighs in at about a kilo or slightly more, and the green, almost black-skinned Gem Store, which reaches the size of an ambitious tennis ball when mature. Like their newly posh relation, the butternut, they will store in a cool place right through until late winter.

By the middle of May, the early potatoes will be producing lots of foliage and the process of tuber production will be well under way, hidden beneath the ground. At this point, it's traditional to start 'earthing up', which means scraping away at the soil between the rows with a hoe and drawing it in over the base of the potato plants. This will prevent tubers near the surface being exposed to the light that makes them green, and according to some, will increase the yield.

At the end of the month, it's time to plant some of the brassicas outside that were sown under cover. Brussels sprouts need a very long spell in the ground in order to produce those little cabbage-like things which Christmas wouldn't be the same without. We grow an F[1] hybrid variety called Trafalgar that crops in good time for the festive season and, even better, tastes really good when carefully cooked.

We plant Brussels sprouts three feet apart with four feet between the rows and – this is really important – we don't dig the ground into which they are planted. It's usually where the onions grew the year before and it's very firm, which is what sprouts like. We excavate a little hole and pop in the seedling, taking care to firm the earth again with a decisive heel. After that, they look after themselves. Some people stake them, but they'll put up with being ignored; ours lean drunkenly this way and that but they still produce a fine crop.

The same goes for all brassicas, more or less. They like firm ground and aren't fussy. Savoys are the one cabbage we insist on growing every year and it is the very definition of winter veg, perhaps being the most forgiving of all.

But there is one problem that afflicts virtually every member of the cabbage tribe: caterpillars. The larva of the cabbage white butterfly will make a meal of any brassica in no time. Of course, you can try using a fine mesh net, but we find there's no substitute for going out each day during the summer and autumn and squashing the little wretches; definitely not nice, but it works.

Our gooseberry patch was planted by our predecessors over twenty years ago, and the bushes seem content to go on fruiting without any great encouragement beyond occasional pruning to keep them in shape. I'm sure we could produce prize-winning fruit with a bit of effort, but to be honest, it's very pleasant to have such undemanding plants that deliver exactly what we need in early summer.

recipes

May is the month when we hold our breath and tighten our belts. The beginning of May is still the Hungry Gap and whatever is in the garden is looking the worse for wear. Later in the month there will be gooseberries, elderflowers and asparagus to remind us that summer is coming.

However, the polytunnel is giving us our first taste of summer. The first indoor broad beans, peas, carrots, radishes and lettuces will be ready. New potatoes will also be eagerly awaited. To do anything more than wash, steam and toss these infant vegetables in butter would be a waste of growing them. They are so tender and flavoursome at this time of year, it's all they need. We tend to have the carrots and radishes raw with a sprinkle of salt or some homemade mayonnaise.

Young broad beans steamed until their tender skins split, served with a knob of butter and perhaps a little pepper, make a first course that most restaurants would consider too simple for their diners. We like food this simple because we know what it takes to produce.

broad bean soup

Serves 4

We tend not to have this soup until the end of May, when the first crop of beans is coming to an end. If there is a good crop, we blanch the extra beans in boiling water for 2 minutes and quickly cool in very cold water before draining and freezing in 1 litre tubs, which hold about 500 g (18 oz).

750 ml (1 pint 5 fl oz) stock

500 g (1 lb 2 oz) broad beans out of their pods

1 onion

2 cloves of garlic

3 tbsp oil

Bring the stock to the boil in a large pot and throw in the beans. Bring back to the boil and simmer for 2–3 minutes.

Peel and slice the onion and garlic. Heat the oil in a frying pan and gently cook the onion and garlic until soft.

If the beans have developed thick skins, remove them from the stock, then skin and return to the stock. Add the onion and garlic to the beans and stock. Simmer until the beans are soft and then purée. Reheat and serve with a dollop of whipped cream and a sprinkling of chopped herbs.

cavolo nero and pine nut sauce for pasta

Serves 4

This is one of the early May dishes that uses what is left of the greens, but is also good in early winter when the cavalo nero is getting started. Any cabbagey greens or chard leaves can be used, so long as they are cut thinly and cooked quickly. Sometimes we fry small cubes of streaky bacon instead of the pine nuts and then it becomes 'bacon and cabbage pasta sauce'. Delicious, but not quite as tasty sounding.

16 cavolo nero leaves
1 large onion
2 cloves of garlic
8 tbsp pine nuts
2 tbsp olive oil
100 ml (4 fl oz) cream
large knob of butter
50 g (2 oz) parmesan, grated
salt and pepper
350–400 g (12–14 oz) pasta

Put a large pot of salted water on to boil for the pasta. Wash the cavolo nero leaves and shake off the excess water. Cut the green leafy bit away from the mid-rib and shred the greens into narrow ribbons. Peel and thinly slice the onion and garlic.

Heat a dry frying pan on a medium heat and toast the pine nuts until golden. Remove the pine nuts and add the oil to the pan. Add the onion and garlic and cook until soft. Stir in the cavolo nero greens and cover with a lid. Leave to cook for 2–3 minutes.

Remove the lid and turn up the heat to boil off any extra moisture, stirring so that the leaves don't catch. When almost dry, take off the heat and add the cream, butter and parmesan. Season with salt and pepper.

Cook the pasta in the boiling water and drain well. While you are draining the pasta, reheat the sauce to just under boiling and mix with the hot pasta. Serve with extra parmesan.

green salads

It seems daft to give a recipe for 'a green salad', but over the years of ordering green/side salads in restaurants, we have been amazed at the variations that have arrived, from the perfectly dressed bowl of fresh green lettuce leaves, through to a tiny side plate piled high with icy cold iceberg, watery cucumber and oxidised onion dressed with white vinegar and nondescript vegetable oil, to sadly limp Lollo Rosso and Oak Leaf lettuces that should have been composted yesterday, mixed with three colours of sliced peppers, cucumber and rancid red onion dressed in a gloopy liquid flecked with 'herbs and spices'.

Then there are starter salads and main course salads – the Greek salad in January that contains no feta and unripe, orange tomatoes, the chicken Caesar salad with blue cheese and bacon or the Salad Niçoise with cheap tuna, gray-ringed hard-boiled eggs and khaki French beans.

Okay, we know you're thinking that we're a bit finicky, but once you've grown and picked your own salad to go straight into the bowl, you, too, will become choosier.

Start with a cut-and-come-again mix such as 'Salad Bowl' and a short row of rocket. A window box or pots will do if space is lacking. Then move on to Little Gems, Cos, Oak Leaf and Butterhead varieties. We grow herbs such as parsley, chives, salad burnett, chervil, sorrel, nasturtiums and coriander to add to salads, and pot marigold for their flowers.

When we pick a bowl of loose-leaf lettuce and herbs to finish a meal, we don't always wash it, just check through it for any dirt and wildlife, then cover it with damp kitchen paper and leave in the fridge until needed. If the whole bowl is going to be eaten, it will be dressed, otherwise the dressing is passed round in a jar. Any leftover undressed salad can be kept in a covered container with some damp kitchen paper in the fridge.

Whole lettuces just have their dirty outside leaves rinsed and spun dry in a salad spinner. Try not to overcrowd the spinner basket, as this bruises the leaves. A good way of reviving limp salad is to wash it in cold water with half a teaspoon of salt and shake it dry, then leave it in the fridge covered with damp kitchen paper in a closed container.

It is sometimes hard to know how much salad to allow per person. What else is being served and the time of day are things to take into account. If you're unsure whether or not people will want onions or scallions, serve these on the side. Eight to 12 leaves per person, depending on size, usually does the trick.

A bowl of home-grown salad brought to the table, dressed there and then, and served on clean plates either after the plainest of omelettes or most special of main courses will be most welcome.

salad dressings

Sometimes all a salad needs is a squeeze of lemon and a drizzle of oil, while at other times a proper dressing is vital. Dressings are very personal: one of us likes lots of mustard, the other lots of garlic. So we compromise – when one makes dressing, mustard is added, and then when the dressing needs topping up, the other adds garlic. Thus we end up with a mustardy/garlicky dressing.

compromise dressing

4 tbsp (60 ml) white wine vinegar
  or cider vinegar

salt

½ tsp grainy mustard

1 clove of garlic

12 tbsp (180 ml) extra virgin olive
  oil

Mix the vinegar and a pinch of salt in a lidded jar until the salt dissolves, then add the mustard. Bruise the garlic with the flat of a large knife and pop into the jar. Add the oil, cover tightly and shake well. Depending on how salty you like your dressing, vary the size of the pinch of salt. The garlic flavour improves with keeping, but don't forget to replace it when topping up the dressing.

asian dressing

We use this dressing for a mix of salad leaves, bean sprouts, scallions and thin strips of cucumber and carrot, made by running a swivel peeler the length of both. All topped with thin slices of rare beef and toasted sesame seeds.

zest and juice of 1 lime

1 small chilli

slice of ginger or galangal, peeled

1 stalk of lemongrass

1 dessertspoon nam pla (Thai fish
  sauce)

2 tbsp rice wine vinegar or cider
  vinegar

1 dessertspoon soy sauce

1 tsp honey or caster sugar
  (optional)

1 tbsp toasted sesame oil

8 tbsp peanut or sunflower oil

Remove the zest from the lime with a zester or a potato peeler and squeeze out the juice. Cut the chilli open long ways. Remove the seeds and membrane that is attached to the chilli flesh for a milder spiciness, or leave in for the full effect. Cut the ginger or galangal into narrow strips and chop the lemongrass.

Put the nam pla, vinegar, soy sauce and sugar or honey into a small pot and warm until the sugar or honey dissolves, then add the chilli, ginger or galangal, lemongrass and lime zest. Remove from the heat and leave to infuse for 5–10 minutes.

Add the lime juice and oils and whisk well. Taste and season if necessary. Leave to cool completely and strain into a bottle or jar. With time you'll find which combination of chilli, ginger, galangal, lime zest and lemongrass you like best, so don't be bound by the above dressing; it's just a base to start from.

blue cheese dressing

This is best with the tougher Little Gem and Cos-type lettuces, as it is quite creamy. Later in the summer, when the pears are ripe, we mix in some toasted walnuts and cubes of ripe pear and it becomes a meal in itself.

3 tbsp mayonnaise

50 g (2 oz) blue cheese (approx.), such as Cashel or Crozier

juice of ½ lemon

olive oil

Mash the mayonnaise and blue cheese together and thin with the lemon juice. If it gets too thin, add some oil to get a coating consistency. Taste and season. Make sure the salad is very dry before dressing.

caesar salad

Serves 2

This is the simplest version of this salad and we feel it's the best way to show off really fresh Cos lettuce.

1 large slice of stale bread
6 tbsp olive oil
1–2 cloves of garlic, grated
1 large head of Cos lettuce
1 tsp Worcestershire sauce
40 g (1½ oz) parmesan cheese, finely grated

Cut the bread into 1 cm (½ inch) cubes and mix with two spoonfuls of the oil and all of the garlic. Wash the lettuce and dry well. Mix the rest of the oil and the Worcestershire sauce in the bottom of a salad bowl, add the parmesan and whisk together. Put the bread, oil and garlic mix in a frying pan on a gentle heat and fry the bread until it's golden on all sides. Drain the bread cubes on kitchen paper. Put the lettuce into the salad bowl and toss with the dressing, add the bread and serve.

beef stew with cobbler topping

Serves 6

A warm May, like a warm September, shortens the winter considerably, but a cold May is not good for the garden or gardener. A comforting stew is sometimes needed, but not with potatoes. Main crop potatoes are past their best and sprouting, and the new ones aren't ready yet, so we use this savoury scone dough as a topping to the stew.

2 onions

1 carrot

2 sticks of celery

2 cloves of garlic

1 kg (2 lb) stewing beef

100 g (4 oz) streaky rashers (about 4)

5 tbsp oil

330 ml (10 fl oz) Smithwicks beer

Warm the oven to GM3/170°C/340°F.

Peel and halve the onions, then thinly slice. Peel the carrot and cut into small dice. Cut the celery into small dice. Peel and slice the garlic. Trim the beef and cut into 2–3 cm (1 inch) cubes. Cut the rashers into narrow strips.

Heat 3 tablespoons of the oil in a heavy casserole over a moderate to high heat. Brown the rasher pieces. When browned, scoop out with a slotted spoon, leaving as much fat as possible. Turn up the heat, add the beef in with the fat and brown also. You may need to do this in a few batches so as not to overcrowd the pan and reduce the heat too much. Remove the browned beef with a slotted spoon.

Add the other 2 tablespoons of oil to the casserole and throw in the onions, carrot, celery and garlic. Turn down the heat to medium and let the vegetables soften. When you stir, make sure to scrape up the brown goo from the meat in the bottom of the casserole. As soon as the vegetables are soft, add the meat and rashers back into the casserole, pour in the Smithwicks and season with pepper. Bring the casserole to the boil, stir and cover.

Transfer to the oven and cook for 3 hours. Remove the stew from the oven and turn up the heat to GM5/190°C/375°F. Take the lid off, lay the dough circles around the edge and brush the tops with egg wash. (You could also add a little more milk to the jug you mixed the egg and milk in and use that.) Return to the oven for 25–30 minutes.

cobbler topping

This is really a savoury scone mix which is put around the edge of the stew while it finishes cooking. The tops of the scones puff up and brown while their bottoms absorb some of the gravy. Sometimes we use this scone mix without the horseradish to make savoury scones to go with soup; just make them thicker and bake at GM6/200°C/400°F for about 20 minutes.

150 g (5 oz) fine wholemeal flour
80 g (3 oz) plain white flour
1 rounded tsp baking powder
50 g (2 oz) butter
2 tbsp parsley, chopped
1 tbsp horseradish, grated
pinch of salt
1 egg
milk

Sift the flours and baking power into a bowl, adding the remaining bran from the sieve. Rub the butter into the flour and stir in the parsley, horseradish and a pinch of salt.

Break the egg into a measuring jug and add enough milk to make 100 ml (3½ fl oz) of liquid. Stir the egg and milk into the flour and mix to a soft dough. Sometimes a little more milk may be needed.

Turn the dough out on a floured surface and pat into a flat shape about 1½ to 2 cm (³/₄ inch) thick and cut into 12 rounds with a 7 cm (3 inch) scone cutter.

gooseberry and elderflower fool

Serves 6

Tart gooseberries are the first true fruit of summer and are complemented by the scent of elderflowers, which bloom at the same time. We find 1 litre ice cream tubs to be perfect for picking soft fruit into. The fruit can be used straight away or the lid put on, labelled and popped into the freezer. We freeze 1 litre tubs of gooseberries with elderflower heads in with them to make this fool in the winter. Any that are left over in the freezer are made into jam after the flower stalks are removed.

850 ml (1½ pints) ripe
  gooseberries
4–6 elderflower heads
50 ml (2 fl oz) water
6 tbsp sugar
270 ml (10 fl oz) cream

Put the gooseberries, elderflower heads, water and sugar into a saucepan. Count the flower heads as they go into the pan so that you can fish out all the stalks when the gooseberries are cooked. Bring the pan to the boil and simmer the gooseberries for 15–20 minutes, until soft. Taste the gooseberries and add more sugar if needed. Leave to cool.

Whip the cream until it is just gone past floppy, but not stiff. Fish the elderflower stalks out of the gooseberries and gently fold the gooseberries into the cream.

gooseberry jam

Makes about 6 jars

If we are using frozen gooseberries with elderflowers, we remove the flower stalks with a fork while the fruit is softening. Unripe gooseberries make a stiffer jam. If we're lucky and net the gooseberry bushes in time, we can let some of the gooseberries ripen to a sweetness that doesn't pucker the mouth.

1 kg (2 lb) gooseberries

400 ml (14 fl oz) water

1.25 kg (2 lb 10 oz) sugar

For hints and tips on jam making, see Seville Orange Marmalade, pp. 26–7.

Top and tail the gooseberries and put into a large pot with the water. Place on a low heat and bring to the boil, then simmer until the fruit is bursting and soft. Put the pot into the bottom oven or a low oven (GM2/150°C/300°F) and check it after 20 minutes.

If you don't like whole berries in your jam, mash the contents of the pot with a potato masher to break up the berries. When the gooseberries are soft, add the sugar and stir until dissolved. Turn up the heat and bring to the boil.

Put the jam jars into a low oven at GM1/140°C/285°F to sterilise and warm them.

Boil the jam for 10 minutes and test for setting (see pp. 26–7) by putting a little jam on a cold saucer in the fridge and leaving it for a few minutes, then push the jam with your finger. If it wrinkles, it's ready. If it's not ready, boil the jam for another 5 minutes and test again.

Take the pot off the heat and let it cool for 10–15 minutes. Pour the jam into the hot jars and cover.

elderflower cordial

Elderflowers herald the coming of summer, their creamy froth decorating hedgerows. Elderflower scent may be captured in this cordial if the weather is sunny and the flowers haven't been open too long. It all depends on the type of May we're having.

30–40 elderflower heads

4 lemons, sliced

1.25 litres (2 pints 4 fl oz) boiling water

1.5 kg (3 lb 3 oz) sugar

60 g (2 oz) citric acid

Put the flowers and lemons into a bowl and pour in the boiling water. Add the sugar and citric acid. Stir until the sugar dissolves. Cover and leave to infuse for 3–4 days. Stir the mix each day, giving the lemons a good mashing.

Strain the liquid into 3 or 4 very clean bottles. If you make more than one batch of this cordial, it may be frozen for later in the summer. We find that after the excitement of the first bottles, it sometimes languishes forgotten in the fridge and then grows a pretty blue mould on the surface. The mould doesn't do any harm but can give an off taste, so we freeze it in three-quarters-full plastic bottles.

june

garden

So much of vegetable growing is about thinking ahead. In June, the first flush of the new season is starting with peas and baby carrots, the very first of the potatoes, a courgette or two from the polytunnel and the broad beans that were sown way back in February. You have to plan ahead.

As the first row of the new potatoes gets dug, we don't hang about. The earth is turned over with a fork and trodden down and then the earliest of the purple sprouting broccoli, a variety called Rudolph that was sown inside in March, is planted in order to get off to a racing start. In a good year, this will mean that our first purple sprouting broccoli will be ready for picking by the end of November.

The first of the early leeks go in too, ready to enjoy the well-cultivated and well-fed soil left by the spuds. Once again, the soil is turned over and firmed down. The leek seedlings are thoroughly watered an hour or more before they are lifted. Then we make holes with a dibber – or you can use the handle of a rake – about five or six inches deep and eight inches apart. A leek seedling is dropped into each hole and the hole is then filled with water. This settles the roots and provides a nice moist start. The deep planting will blanch a good portion of each leek so that, when they are ready to be lifted later in the year, we will get more white than green in the stem.

There is something immensely satisfying about planting leeks; it imposes a kind of neatness and discipline on even the messiest gardeners, and there is the realisation that the process will really pay dividends when the spindly little seedlings have bulked up into something delicious.

Leek planting can be staggered. The early-maturing varieties need to be planted first, ideally by mid-June, but leeks in general can be planted well into August if you don't mind waiting a bit longer for the harvest.

Although by June our cut-and-come-again lettuces, sown in the polytunnel in February, are reaching for the sky, they will still be producing very edible salad. But from March, we will have been sowing lettuces in modules roughly every fortnight, and most of these, planted out in the polytunnel, will have grown to maturity there. However, from early June we plant lettuces outside, where they grow more slowly but develop even better flavour.

Lettuce can be grown outdoors virtually all year round if you choose the varieties with care. They are slugs' favourite food, but thanks to plenty of frogs and the odd hedgehog, we aren't hugely troubled by these pesky mollusks, and starting our outdoor lettuce under cover seems to afford an extra degree of protection. Some people claim that their lettuce 'never came up', but it's much more likely that it did and a single slug devoured the whole lot within 15 minutes. Slugs are quicker than you might think.

The end of June generally sees our first cucumber reach edible size and after that they seem to appear overnight. But tomatoes, which are generally regarded as hardier and less demanding, take a little longer.

Strawberries are, in a sense, the key crop for June in that they seem to represent what summer is all about. We are still novice growers, trying to find the ideal variety with a proper old-fashioned flavour. In terms of cultivation, though, they are pretty easy. We plant in the autumn and, after fruiting the following summer, we peg down the shoots that are then produced. In a few weeks, these will have produced new plants which can be potted, ready for planting later in the year. The old ones are discarded. And so it goes on.

If strawberries are the essence of summer in terms of fruit, asparagus must be the vegetable equivalent. It requires patience, but an asparagus bed will last for twenty years or more, which makes it a good investment.

Most people plant asparagus crowns in late spring in well-drained soil a couple of feet apart. Asparagus must be allowed to get properly established before any spears can be cut, and this involves the painful process of spending two whole seasons resisting the temptation to pick. In year three, you can take a couple of stalks per plant, but twelve months later it's permitted to gobble up the whole lot – but only until the end of June, at which stage the plants must be allowed to regain their energy by producing foliage.

Somewhat unusually, we grew our asparagus from seed, which is supposed to be very difficult, but we seem to have been exceptionally lucky. Growing from seed has the benefit of allowing you to harvest one stalk per plant in the second year, which meant a whopping twelve asparagus spears to be eaten a little more than a year after the seed was sown. And it gets better!

recipes

June is the month when the garden really begins to take off, but the polytunnel is a wonderful bonus. The courgettes in the tunnel will start to do their thing. After the excitement of the first few, we find ourselves overrun. Courgette flowers are edible; the petals sliced off and torn into strips are added to the flesh almost at the end of cooking.

Any male flowers that are fresh are used too. If there are enough flowers, we might treat ourselves to them dipped in a light batter and deep fried. Be careful to check any closed flowers, or you could end up with deep-fried butterfly, as we once did! It was a Meadow Brown. Pumpkin and squash flowers can be used in the same way later in the summer.

Asparagus is another June vegetable that needs nothing more than a little butter after brief cooking to make it a star. We like parmesan shaved over it and a hollandaise is richly delicious, but for the first pickings we keep it low key.

pea and mint soup

The best way to eat home-grown peas is as tiny petits pois on their own, with nothing but a little butter and pepper. The ones that elude you at this stage and grow up to produce slightly wrinkly pods are best as soup. Of course, if you're feeling very thrifty, you can make the soup with just the pods from the petits pois. Whole overgrown mangetout peas work well too.

1 onion

1 tbsp oil

500 g (1 lb 2 oz) peas in their pods

500–750 ml (1–1¼ pints) water or stock

4 sprigs of mint

salt and pepper

Finely slice the onion and cook until soft in the oil. If you have lots of peas, pod them and add to the pot. If you have a few peas and want to make the most of them, add any pods that are still smooth. Pour in enough water or stock to come up to the top of the peas and add two sprigs of mint. Bring to the boil, then turn down the heat and simmer until the peas are soft. Take off the heat and cool.

Remove the mint sprigs and liquidise. If you have used pods, push through a sieve or Mouli Legumes to remove any fibrous pieces of pod.

Clean the pot and return the soup to it, thin with water or stock to the runniness you desire and bring back to the boil. Taste and adjust seasoning. Chop the leaves from the other two mint sprigs and add to the pot, then serve.

byessar

Serves 6

Tiny broad beans are delicious on their own eaten like Smarties, but when they get bigger they need to be blanched and skinned. They freeze very well like this; we freeze them in ice cream tubs.

500 g (1 lb) broad beans, podded and skinned

2 cloves of garlic, chopped

1 tsp ground cumin

1 tsp fresh oregano leaves, chopped

salt and pepper

100 ml (3 fl oz) olive oil

lemon juice

Cook the broad beans gently with half a cup of water. When soft, transfer to a food processor and add the garlic, cumin, oregano and some salt and pepper. Process until smooth, then add the olive oil in a thin stream (as if you were making mayonnaise). It will absorb more oil if you want to be generous.

Taste and season with more salt, pepper and lemon juice if required. It looks very like an avocado dip and has a beautiful colour. It's also very moreish. Serve with raw vegetables and toasted pittas.

risotto primavera

Our risottos tend to reflect what's on offer in the tunnel, a proper primavera of young courgettes, courgette flowers, herbs, peas and beans. Rather than stretching the first pickings of May, they take centre stage. Wild garlic, which grows in our woods, is a native plant and has broad leaves and flowers in a ball at the end of a stalk. It flowers in May and early June depending on the weather and is a welcome addition to this risotto.

850 ml (1 ½ pints) stock

1 onion

1 clove of garlic

1 small carrot

1 small stick of celery

2–3 small courgettes and their flowers

2–3 handfuls of very young broad beans/peas/French beans

asparagus spears

2 tbsp olive oil

285 g (10 oz) carnaroli rice

200 ml (7 fl oz) dry white wine

6 wild garlic leaves

2 wild garlic flower heads

60 g (2 oz) parmesan, grated

30 g (1 oz) butter

salt and pepper

Put the stock in a pot and keep on the heat. Peel and finely dice the onion, garlic, carrot and celery. Trim the courgettes and cut into thin rounds. Tear the yellow courgette petals into strips. String the French beans, trim the asparagus spears and cut into short lengths. If the beans and asparagus are older, they may need to be blanched for 2 minutes before adding to the risotto.

Heat the oil in a deep, wide frying pan and soften the onion, carrot, celery and garlic over a moderate heat. Add the rice to the pan and coat it well with the fat. Turn up the heat and add the wine, letting it bubble for a minute to evaporate the alcohol. Stir. Turn down the heat to a moderate simmer, not too slow. Keep stirring.

When the rice is just starting to stick, add a ladle of hot stock. Keep stirring. As each ladleful is absorbed, add another. Keep stirring. The rice is done when it looks translucent and the chalky bit has gone from the middle. Keep stirring. About 10 minutes after the wine goes in, add the courgettes, beans and asparagus. Add more stock as necessary until the rice is done.

Chop the wild garlic leaves into fine ribbons and separate the flowers from the stalks. Add to the risotto with the cheese and butter. Stir through and take off the heat. Serve in warm bowls with extra parmesan.

courgette and herb frittata

Serves 4

We use chopped parsley when the courgettes are first ready, but later in the summer we use tarragon, which has a mild aniseed flavour.

3 courgettes
1 onion, sliced
1 clove garlic, chopped
oil
5 eggs
salt and pepper
2 tbsp parmesan, grated
3 tbsp herbs, chopped
butter

Three courgettes is a bit arbitrary, we know, but it depends on their size. Medium is what you need here, not the monsters that have escaped from a giant marrow competition. Wash and slice the courgettes. Cook the onion and garlic in a little oil until soft, then cook the sliced courgettes until they start to brown.

Break the eggs into a bowl and mix well with a fork until the yolks and whites are amalgamated. Add salt and pepper. Add the cooked onion, garlic, courgettes, parmesan and the chopped herbs.

Melt some butter in a frying pan and add the egg mixture. Cook on a medium heat until golden underneath and finish the top under the grill (or turn it out and finish on the pan). Leave to cool before cutting.

herby new potato salad

Serves 6

The new potatoes available in June are best steamed and served with butter. We regularly do too many on purpose so we can have them the next day as potato salad, either dressed with a herby vinaigrette dressing or mayonnaise stirred through with sliced radishes and capers. However, not all the family like capers. Poreens are the small potatoes that are fiddly to wash but make the best salad when split in half and mixed with dressing.

3 tbsp herbs (parsley, chives and mint), chopped
1 tsp wholegrain mustard
2 tbsp lemon juice
salt and pepper
60–80 ml (2–3 fl oz) olive oil
500 g (1 lb 2 oz) potatoes, cooked, preferably still warm

Put the herbs, mustard, lemon juice, pinch of salt and oil into a bowl and mix together. Cut the potatoes into bite-sized pieces into the bowl. Grind in some pepper. Gently stir the potatoes through the dressing. Taste and adjust seasoning. Leave to cool.

The proportions and types of herbs can be adjusted to your taste and mood; some days more onion in the form of scallions is needed, or in our case there is always lots of coriander in the polytunnel. This is just a starting point. Make it your own.

potato salad with radish and capers

Homemade mayonnaise is wonderful, but you can't always use it, nor do you have the time to make it. A jar of good shop mayonnaise can be tarted up with a squeeze of lemon, a glug or two of olive oil, garlic or mustard so that anyone who can't have raw egg is safe.

500 g (1 lb 2 oz) cooked new potatoes
5 long radishes, or more if the round type
1 shallot
2 tbsp drained capers
mayonnaise
salt and pepper

Cut the potatoes into bite-sized pieces. Wash and slice the radishes into rounds. Peel and thinly slice the shallot. Gently mix all these with the capers in a bowl and add enough mayonnaise to lubricate. Taste and season.

mayonnaise

Everything for making mayonnaise should be at room temperature, so don't try this in January if you live in a cold house. If you keep your eggs, lemons and oil in the fridge, take them out well in advance to warm up. Olive oil goes cloudy when it gets too cold. Good-quality extra virgin olive oil makes a dark green, strongly flavoured mayonnaise, great for dipping baby vegetables in, but would be lost with strong flavours such as radishes and capers.

1 egg yolk
½ tsp dry mustard powder
salt and pepper
180 ml (6 fl oz) mix of olive and sunflower oil
juice of ½ lemon

In a clean bowl, whisk together the egg yolk, mustard powder and a pinch of salt. When there are no more lumps of mustard, add a teaspoon of oil and whisk it in. Keep adding the oil in teaspoonfuls, making sure it is well whisked in before adding the next. As the mayonnaise thickens, add more oil each time. After about half the oil has been added, squeeze in some of the lemon juice and whisk it through well. Keep adding the oil and lemon until all the oil is used. Taste the mayonnaise and add more lemon, salt and pepper, as you like.

lamb kebabs

Serves 6

The coriander in the polytunnel runs to seed after some time and the green seeds have a delicious fresh taste. We sometimes use them gently bruised in salads and stir-fries. We also collect the plants as the first seeds turn brown and dry them in bunches, seed heads down, in paper bags. When the seeds have ripened, we collect them to use for kebabs and in curries.

1 tbsp cumin seed

2 tbsp coriander seeds

3 cloves of garlic

1 tsp ground cinnamon

juice of $\frac{1}{2}$ lemon

3 tbsp olive oil

salt and pepper

700 g (1 lb 8 oz) lean lamb, leg or
   chump chops

Toast the cumin and coriander seeds in a dry pan over a medium heat until they start to give off their scent and begin to colour. Leave to cool. Meanwhile, peel the garlic, then grate into a ceramic bowl. Grind the cumin and coriander together in a mortar and pestle or a coffee grinder and add to the garlic. Mix in the cinnamon, lemon juice, oil, salt and pepper.

Cut the lamb into 1 $\frac{1}{2}$ cm ($\frac{1}{2}$ inch) cubes and mix with the garlic and spice mix. Leave covered for as long as you can, ideally overnight but for at least half an hour. Thread onto metal skewers and cook on the barbecue or under the grill, turning regularly. These are really good in a pitta with a yoghurt dressing with lots of salad.

summer birthday cake

We have three birthdays to be celebrated through the summer, so a simple sponge with cream and fresh fruit makes a perfect birthday cake. The fruit is replaced with jam in the winter.

3 eggs

85 g (3 oz) caster sugar

85 g (3 oz) plain flour

180 ml (6 fl oz) cream

medium-sized punnet of fresh strawberries

1–2 tbsp sugar

Set the oven to GM5/190°C/375°F. Line and grease two round, shallow 18 cm (7 inch) cake tins with paper.

Put the eggs and sugar into a bowl. Whisk together with an electric whisk until very pale and there is a ribbon of froth on top when the whisk is taken out.

Sift the flour and add half to the eggs and sugar. Fold the flour into the eggs very gently with a spoon and do the same with the rest of the flour. Mix through evenly, then divide the mixture between the cake tins and bake in the centre of the oven for 15–20 minutes.

The cakes will have shrunk from the sides of the tin and the top will spring back when gently poked with a finger. Remove the cakes from the tins to a wire rack and peel off the lining paper. Leave to cool.

Whip the cream. Halve the berries, except for the best one. Sprinkle the halved berries with sugar to draw out the flavour. Arrange half the berries onto one of the sponge layers and top with half the cream. Put the other sponge on top, covered by a layer of berries and then the rest of the cream. Top with the perfect strawberry and birthday candles.

strawberry jam

Makes about 7 jars

Don't expect this jam to be stiff. It's a runny jam best eaten within a month or two of being made. I use ordinary granulated sugar for jam and find it works fine. Get your jars and lids ready on a baking tray and put a saucer into the fridge while the strawberries are softening. When you start to test the jam for its setting point (see pp. 26–7), put the jars into the oven at GM1/140°C/285°F or the simmering oven of the Aga.

1.6 kg (3 lb 8 oz) strawberries, cleaned

juice of ½ lemon

1.4 kg (3 lb) sugar

For hint and tips on jam making, see Seville Orange Marmalade, pp. 26–7.

Put the strawberries and the lemon juice into a large pot on a low heat. When the juice starts to run, turn up the heat, bring to a simmer and cook the berries until soft. (I put the pot on the floor of the bottom oven of the Aga to simmer.) This will take about 20–30 minutes.

When soft, turn down the heat and add the sugar. Stir until the sugar has dissolved. Turn up the heat and bring to the boil, then boil fast. Test for the setting point after 10–15 minutes by putting a teaspoonful onto the cold saucer in the fridge and leaving to cool for 3 minutes. Push the cold jam from the edge with your finger. If it wrinkles, the jam will set, otherwise boil for another 5 minutes and try again.

When the jam reaches its setting point, remove from the heat and leave to cool for 10–15 minutes. Pour the jam into the hot sterilised jars and cover with lids or waxed paper and cellophane.

july

garden

The tomatoes are in full flow by mid-July, and the basil, sown under cover in April and planted out between the tomato plants, will be in full leaf. Just as these two plants taste well together, they are also said to make successful companions for each other as they grow. We can't vouch for this, but we tend to grow them together all the same.

The greatest task at this stage, certainly inside and often outside, is watering. In very hot weather, it can take an hour to give the polytunnel a thorough soaking. Outside, the celery and the celeriac get priority because if they don't have plenty of water, they will bolt and run to seed. The onions are much more forgiving but still appreciate water when it's hot, not to mention that the yield improves significantly. Squashes, presumably because they have such a huge area of leaf, sometimes need gallons of water. Fortunately, we have a separate well solely for outside use.

Watering requires a degree of care. If tomatoes or carrots, for example, are thirsty, it's important not to give too much water in one go, otherwise they swell and crack. Little and often is the solution.

July is when we sow our autumn carrots, the ones that will stay in the ground throughout the winter and, with a bit of luck, struggle on until the first of the spring crop is ready in the polytunnel. The secret with autumn carrots is to sow very thinly so that the seedlings need minimal thinning, if any. This is because the carrot fly can smell carrot plants being pulled and will dive in. The only problem is that carrot seeds are very small and it takes a certain amount of optimism to sow so sparingly. The right variety is important too. Our favourite is one called Autumn King Improved, which, given space and time, can bulk up into monsters that are as tasty as they are huge.

This is the one carrot crop that always succumbs, to some extent, to carrot fly damage, but it is generally slight enough to be dealt with by slicing out the affected areas. A bit of fly damage is curiously reassuring when found in commercially grown organic carrots; it shows that they really are chemical free.

Hardy varieties of winter lettuce can be sown in July so as to allow reasonably large growth before the cold weather sets in. Sown now, they should provide good eating in May.

As John Seymour, the apostle of sustainable living, once said, 'The hoe is the herbicide of the future.' In midsummer, if the weather is sunny and dry, hoeing becomes a pleasure rather than a duty. The secret of hoeing is to keep disturbing the top half-inch of the soil so that weed seeds give up and don't bother.

Some weeding is essential, and in both June and July the onion bed and the few rows of shallots need to be attended to by hand. As the onions swell, hoeing can be a tricky business. Even if the bed has been hoed well earlier in the season, the remaining weeds will be infuriatingly close to the onions, hence the need to get down on all fours and pull them out by hand.

By the end of the month, the hard work will be rewarded as the foliage starts to brown and fall over. This is known as harvest time. The onions ripen in the sun and need to be gently pulled and left on the ground for the leaves to wither. Then they can be brought inside and left for a couple of weeks before twisting off the dried leaves and roots and putting them in net bags for storage.

One perennial plant that delivers a great deal of pleasure and with minimal effort is the globe artichoke, which produces big, fleshy flower buds each July. It's possible to grow from seed, but a more dependable approach is to buy plants from the garden centre, or better still, beg a few off-shoots from a friend. They need to be planted, in either spring or autumn, with a lot of well-rotted manure. It's worth lavishing a lot of care on the planting process because globe artichokes will remain productive for as much as ten years; at that stage, simply divide the old plants and start again, placing them four feet apart.

July also sees a huge crop of redcurrants and blackcurrants, which is shared with the local birds, who are simply crazy about them. One of these years we'll get around to protecting at least some of the fruit with netting. Nevertheless, we still manage to pick a reasonable amount.

The currant bushes came with the property and are very well established at this stage. The intricacies of pruning seem very complex, at least according to the textbooks, so we content ourselves with just cutting out old wood and lopping off straggling branches. This isn't the proper way to do it, but I think I would need to be retired to learn the approved method. But hell, it works!

recipes

Once July comes, both the tunnel and garden are in full swing and the currants ripen. We have red, black and white currants and because they aren't netted it's a race between us and the birds to pick the most. So far, the birds are winning on the red and white front, but we still get enough to make a few tarts and a pot or two of jelly. We do better with the blackcurrants, stewing them with sugar or honey and folding them into whipped cream to make a fool when cold.

Though most of the currants we pick are stowed in the freezer to turn into jam or jelly in the winter, we make a few pots to see us through the summer. We find there's more than enough to do in the summer than stand over a pan of jam on the Aga, so we save it for a rainy day.

Summer raspberries are a target for the birds too, but we do get some of them and, along with redcurrants and blackcurrants, they can be heated with sugar until the juice runs and made into summer pudding.

We wait in great anticipation for the first cucumber and tomatoes. The first cucumber is reserved for cucumber sandwiches – thinly sliced cucumber in buttered white sliced pan sprinkled with salt and pepper, and crusts removed, of course. With warm scones, fresh jam and cream, these sandwiches are afternoon tea's *raison d'être*.

gazpacho

Serves 6

This is definitely a polytunnel soup, or perhaps a puréed salad – and all the better for properly ripe tomatoes. It's best fresh, but it can be made in advance to let the flavours develop. If keeping overnight, it might be best not to add the garlic until about an hour before serving. Use a fine grater and stir through.

1 onion, chopped

2 cloves of garlic, chopped

500 g (1 lb 2 oz) tomatoes, skinned and chopped

1 cucumber, peeled and chopped

wine vinegar or lemon juice

olive oil

salt and pepper

chilled water

1 small green pepper

1 cm ($\frac{1}{2}$ inch) thick slice of cucumber

1 tomato

coriander leaves, chopped

Whiz the onion, garlic, tomatoes and cucumber in a food processor or liquidiser until smooth; you may have to do it in batches. Pour into a jug and taste. Season with the vinegar/ lemon juice, oil, salt and pepper and chill. Add some ice cubes to speed up the process. Before serving, stir and taste, adding more salt if necessary and enough chilled water to make it soup-like.

Halve the pepper and remove the seeds. Finely dice. Peel and deseed the extra cucumber and tomato. Finely dice the flesh. Pour the soup into bowls and sprinkle with the coriander, pepper, cucumber and tomato.

tomato salad #1

Serves 4

Eating a ripe tomato from the plant which is still warm from the tunnel is bliss. We have never had a shop tomato that has tasted the same.

Tomato salad is July to us; we slice them horizontally and sprinkle over some olive oil, salt and pepper. Perfect with everything from a fillet of sole, quiche, barbecued leg of lamb to slices of mozzarella, it's a meal in itself. Tomatoes for salad should be warm from the sun, not chilly from the fridge.

1 clove of garlic
8–12 ripe tomatoes
salt
10–12 basil leaves
4 tbsp really good olive oil
pepper

This is one time when a really subtle hand with the garlic is necessary. Skin the garlic clove and cut in half lengthways. Rub the cut sides of the garlic around four plates.

Thinly slice the tomatoes horizontally, about 5 mm ($^1/_4$ inch) thick, discard the top and bottom slices and cut out any green core of the tomato. Lay the tomato slices in a single layer on the plates and sprinkle with a little salt.

Remove the basil leaves from the stalks and tear the larger ones into quarters. Evenly distribute between the four plates. Pour a tablespoon of olive oil over each plate and grind on a little black pepper. Leave in the sunshine or a warm spot for 15 minutes to let the flavours mellow. Serve with some bread to mop up the juice.

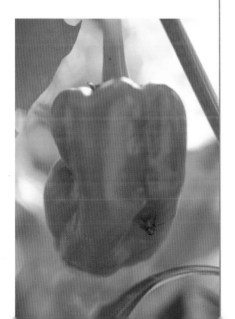

tomato salad #2

This is a more rugged version of Tomato Salad #1 and is served in a bowl with a main course.

8–12 tomatoes
2 cloves of garlic
1 shallot
salt and pepper
4 tbsp olive oil
12 large basil leaves

Halve the tomatoes and cut out the green cores. Cut each half into quarters and put into a bowl with any juice that has escaped. Finely grate the garlic into the bowl or slice it thinly. Peel and slice the shallot into very thin rings and sprinkle over the salad. Season the salad with salt and pepper and gently mix. Add the oil and the basil leaves and stir them in gently.

cucumber salad

Serves 4–6

This looks really pretty with nasturtium and borage flowers around it and a few pot marigold petals sprinkled over the top. All three flowers are easy to grow and will seed themselves and take over, perfect for easy-going gardeners.

1 cucumber

2 tbsp vinegar (cider or white wine will do)

salt

1 tbsp sunflower oil

1 tbsp olive oil

3 sprigs of tarragon

edible flowers

Use a swivel peeler to cut the cucumber into long, thin ribbons, leaving some of the skin on one edge. Discard the soft centre where the seeds are. Mix the vinegar with a pinch of salt and the oils. Take the tarragon leaves off the stalks and mix with the dressing. Pour over the cucumber ribbons and toss gently. Serve in a shallow dish with the flowers around the edge.

tomato and cucumber salad

We can't really give an exact recipe for this. We just chop even quantities of cucumber and tomatoes into similar-sized pieces, pour on some olive oil and a squeeze of lemon.

Sometimes we add torn basil leaves or parsley, sometimes some black olives, feta cheese or Knockalara sheep's cheese and oregano for a Greek-style salad, or we might flake in some tinned tuna and a spoonful of capers. It all depends on our mood and what's available.

fresh tomato sauce

The best tomatoes for this are the thick-fleshed plum or beefsteak ones. It looks more like you are composting than cooking with the round varieties, but if you have a glut, it's worth making. Serve with pasta or on top of a plain grilled steak.

4–6 ripe tomatoes, depending on
   size, per person
salt and pepper
olive oil
garlic
basil

Boil a kettle of water. Put the tomatoes into a heatproof bowl and pour over the boiling water. Leave for a few minutes and when the skins start to split, pour off the water and peel the tomatoes. Halve the tomatoes and remove the seeds. Chop the flesh into small pieces and put into a bowl. Season with salt and pepper and stir in the oil.

Peel and slice the garlic as thinly as possible and stir into the tomato flesh. Tear up half the basil leaves and add. Cover the mixture and leave somewhere warm for a while for the flavours to develop. Before serving, tear up the rest of the basil leaves and add to the sauce.

tzatziki

This sauce is great dolloped onto barbecued lamb and with barbecued vegetables.

1 cucumber, peeled

½ tsp salt

500 g (1 lb 2 oz) tub natural yoghurt

2 cloves of garlic

pepper

4 tbsp fresh mint, chopped

Grate the cucumber and mix with the salt. Leave to drain in a colander for at least 30 minutes. Squeeze out the cucumber and stir into the yoghurt. Finely grate in the garlic. Season with pepper to taste. Chill for 30 minutes and sprinkle with the mint before serving.

globe artichokes

Globe artichokes are large thistle flowers. These wonderful plants should be grown by anyone with a garden. At one time we grew ours against the railings of our front garden. They were a great conversation starter with passers-by, they were photographed by an artistic neighbour and we even had a few stolen.

They grow quite tall and flower in the summer. Then they die back for the winter, leaving a large spray of silvery green leaves. Some varieties produce small flower buds that may be cooked and eaten whole.

Choose 1 large flower or 2 smaller flowers per person; pick the buds while still closed at the centre. Cook in boiling water until one of the green bracts can be pulled off easily. Remove from the heat and drain well in a colander. Serve on a large hot plate with ramekins of hot melted butter.

Eat by pulling off the green bracts one at a time and dipping the fleshy end that was attached to the stalk into the butter and pulling it between your top and bottom teeth to scrape off the flesh. As you work your way around the artichoke, the pile of debris will grow. Towards the centre the bracts will form a pointy cone. Pick this off in one go; only the bottom part will be edible. Underneath there is a hairy 'choke'; this should be removed by scraping it away gently with a teaspoon. The choke is edible only in very small young artichokes. You have now reached the heart of the artichoke. Cut it into quarters or sixths and mix with the last of the butter and eat. This is real slow food!

We like melted butter best with our artichokes, but French dressing is also an option. Don't try to drink wine with artichokes, as it tastes horrible.

If we have a large amount of artichokes ready at the one time, we cook them as follows: trim off the outside bracts and the chokes. Cook in boiling water until tender. Drain. Cut the artichokes in half and place in a single layer into a hot buttered ovenproof dish. Sprinkle with grated parmesan mixed with chopped parsley and breadcrumbs. Brown under the grill.

salad niçoise

This can be put together in 20 minutes. Now, that really is fast food! Nearly all your veg and protein on the one plate, and if you eat it outside you'll even get your vitamin D fix into the bargain.

Per person

6 young thin French beans

1 egg

2 small new spuds

1 anchovy or 1 tsp nam pla (Thai fish sauce)

French dressing

6–8 leaves of Cos or Little Gem lettuce

1½ small ripe tomatoes, quartered

½ can tuna

a few olives

Bring two small to medium pots half-full of water to the boil. Drop the beans into one and when it returns to the boil, scoop them out into a bowl of cold water. Put the eggs into the other pot and bring back to the boil. Simmer the eggs for 10–12 minutes and cool quickly when done. Pop the spuds in the pot the beans came out of and cook until just tender. Peel and quarter the eggs.

Mash the anchovy into the French dressing or add the nam pla and dress the leaves with this. Arrange the dressed leaves on plates and share out the quartered tomatoes, eggs, tuna and spuds. Top with the beans and olives.

barbecue

If the weather is good, eating outside and a barbecue are *de rigueur*. Interesting
sausages, steaks and butterflied leg of lamb all get the chargrill treatment. Even
vegetables aren't safe: whole scallions are brushed with oil and grilled, courgettes
are sliced lengthways, oiled and grilled, dusted with toasted cumin seeds and a
squeeze of lemon, then left to cool. The earliest of the green peppers and
aubergines get similar treatment. Garlic and lemon for the peppers and a smear of
pesto for the aubergines are all that's needed.

We love doing a whole leg of lamb with its bone removed and flattened out like a
'butterfly'. We marinate it with the following.

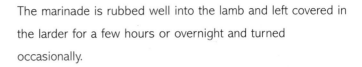

Marinade

juice of 2–3 lemons

6 cloves of garlic, crushed

1 dessertspoon black peppercorns, crushed (more if Tom is in charge) or 2 tbsp toasted cumin and coriander, mixed and crushed

leaves of 5–6 sprigs of thyme

salt

olive oil

The marinade is rubbed well into the lamb and left covered in the larder for a few hours or overnight and turned occasionally.

The barbecue is fired up and we let it get really hot. The bars are oiled and on goes the lamb. When it's browned enough on one side, it's turned over and the other side is browned.

This is where we cheat: we take it off the barbeque and put it in a roasting tin and into the roasting oven of the Aga to finish cooking. The length of time needed in the oven depends on how thick the meat is and how well done we want it: 5–10 minutes for a small new season leg of lamb, 15–20 minutes for one later in the year. We either guess or use a meat thermometer by sticking it into the middle of the thickest part. When it reads 60°–70°C, we take it out and let it rest for 10–15 minutes.

While the lamb is in the oven and the barbecue is free, we cook the vegetables.

We also roll out 60 g (2 oz) pieces of pizza dough into 10 cm (4 inch) rounds and cook them on the grill to have with the lamb and vegetables.

redcurrant tartlets

Makes 18

This is a good way to make a small quantity of home-grown fruit go further. Redcurrants are particularly good, or a mix of red and white. Blackcurrants or raspberries work just as well.

Pastry

110 g (4 oz) butter, cold from the
    fridge
170 g (6 oz) plain flour
1 tbsp caster sugar
1 medium egg, beaten

145 g (5 oz) currants

Custard

2 eggs
20 g (1 oz) plain flour
2 tbsp sugar
170 ml (6 fl oz) approx. cream

Rub the butter into the flour and stir in the sugar. Add enough egg to bind the mixture. Wrap in plastic and leave to rest in the fridge for 20 minutes.

Heat the oven to GM6/200°C/400°F.

Roll out the pastry to 3 cm ($\frac{1}{8}$ inch) thick and cut into 7.5 cm (3 inch) circles. Line bun tins with these. Put a dessertspoonful of currants into each tartlet.

In a measuring jug, whisk the eggs into the flour and sugar. Add enough cream to make the liquid up to 250 ml (8 fl oz). Mix well. Gently add a tablespoonful of the custard to each tartlet.

Bake for 15–20 minutes. Remove the tartlets from the tins to a wire rack and leave to cool to room temperature. Serve with cream.

blackcurrant jam

Makes about 6 jars

We use the simmering oven of the Aga to soften the fruit, though you can also put the pot in a low oven at about GM1/140°C/285°F. Remember to check the fruit regularly.

600 g (1 lb 5 oz) blackcurrants
500 ml (18 fl oz) water
700 g (1 lb 8 oz) sugar
knob of butter or dessertspoon of
  sunflower oil
approx. 6 clean jars and lids

For hints and tips on jam making, see Seville Orange Marmalade, pp. 26–7.

Put the currants and water into a large pot or preserving pan and slowly bring to the boil. Cook until the fruit is soft. Slowly add the sugar and stir until dissolved. Raise the heat and boil until the setting point is reached (see pp. 26–7). Check by putting a spoonful of jam on a cold saucer in the fridge and leaving for a few minutes. If the skin wrinkles when pushed from the edge, it's ready.

While checking for the setting point, put the jars and lids into a low oven to warm through. When the jam is ready, add a knob of butter or a dessertspoon of sunflower oil and stir to disperse the froth. Remove from the heat and leave to stand for 10–15 minutes. Take the jars out of the oven, fill with jam and cover while still hot.

august

garden

Although in gardening terms August is late summer, there is often a faint hint of autumn in the air, especially in contrast with the dog days of July.

The polytunnel is now bursting with natural abundance. We give away hundreds of cucumbers, process tons of tomatoes for the freezer and make occasional batches of chutney. The sweetcorn swells and demands daily watering, the aubergines are black and glossy, the French beans are in full swing and there is a constant need to tie, cut, prune, hoe and simply harvest.

The only crop that is lagging behind is, as always, the peppers. We always choose so-called early varieties, but they still take an age. The little green fruit won't be an edible size until next month and they refuse to go red, so we develop a taste for green peppers and leave a few hanging on the plants until, in December, we harvest something vaguely orange.

Outside, the celeriac is still looking small and sulky, but a great deal of water and liquid manure will ensure that they reach the requisite cricket ball size by autumn. The beetroot, of which I always sow far too much, is burgeoning and, with a bit of luck, the carrot foliage won't be wilting, which is the sure sign of lethal fly damage.

The squashes will have got completely out of hand, trying to climb fences and trees, undeterred by having their furthest tendrils torn up by the lawnmower, still producing more and more fruit to see us into the New Year.

At this stage, it would be easy to bask in the simple abundance of the garden, but that would leave us hungry later on. The big task in the polytunnel, watering aside, is to find room for the salad crops to brighten up the last few months of the year. Space must be found for cut-and-come-again lettuce, rocket and peppery landcress, corn salad and winter purslane.

The apple and pear trees get a regular dose of wood ash to help the ripening process, but unless it has been a chilly summer, supplies of this useful commodity are running low. The children are encouraged to drag fallen branches from our woods into the barn where they can dry out, and I try to remember to get the chainsaw serviced before everyone else gets the same idea.

Having got tired of the ease with which radishes grow at the start of the summer, we will probably sow some now in order to enjoy their peppery crunch and bright red colour. And speaking of colour, a sowing of rainbow chard (in which the stems are variously white, yellow, pink and red) will provide a welcome change from the brassicas and the root crops that dominate the garden throughout the winter. And a couple of rows of hardy scallions, like the Japanese Ishikura, should see us through from October to spring.

Our raspberries are an autumn-fruiting variety (we don't know which one, because they came with the land), but they are usually in full spate from August until October. This is much better than having the usual summer version, because the birds have more to distract them later in the year and you get much more of a crop and for longer.

The only problem lies in remembering to cut the canes back to ground level during the winter. Otherwise, you get fruit from June until October. This may seem like a good arrangement, but the plants will exhaust themselves and after a couple of years there will be no fruit at all.

recipes

August is the best summer month in the vegetable garden; there is fruitfulness everywhere you look. Courgettes turn to marrows in the blink of an eye. There are bowls of tomatoes and plums to be picked every day and the freezer starts to fill with tomato sauces and fruit for the winter. Meat certainly plays second fiddle at this time of year.

The first of the autumn raspberries are ready and the raspberry canes will give us a litre tub practically every day to be eaten or frozen for our favourite jam. Field mushrooms will magically appear in the fields, repaying daily return trips with delicate pink gilled mushrooms for breakfast or, if there are enough, a sauce for pasta. The end of August means the first blackberries, but also the end of the summer holidays and that back-to-school feeling.

roast tomatoes

These are best just after they have cooled down to room temperature. They are slightly sticky and sweet and tend not to last very long, mainly because they are so moreish, but they will hold for a day or two in the fridge. If you are making them in advance and keeping them in the fridge, do take them out ahead of time and let them warm up. Sometimes we add a bulb or two of garlic, broken into cloves, into the tin as well. The roast garlic makes a wonderful spread for crostini.

15–20 tomatoes
garlic
fresh thyme
olive oil
salt and pepper

Heat the oven to GM6/200°C/400°C.

Halve the tomatoes vertically and remove the green core from each half. Place them cut side up in a roasting tin. Pack in as many as you can in a single layer, as they shrink during cooking. Peel and thinly slice the garlic. Put a slice of garlic on each tomato half. Strip the leaves off the thyme and sprinkle them over the tomatoes. Dribble olive oil over the tomatoes and sprinkle with salt and pepper. Roast in the oven for about 50–60 minutes.

roast tomato and celery soup

Serves 6

While there is a glut of summer tomatoes, we will roast extra and make this soup for lunches or freeze it for dismal winter days when we need a lift.

1 head of celery

1 clove of garlic

1 tomato

1 large onion

1.5 litres (2 pints 13 fl oz) boiling water

sprig of thyme

salt and pepper

1 tbsp olive oil

50 g (2 oz) butter

15 medium–large tomatoes, halved and roasted with garlic and thyme (see p. 152)

To make the stock, break the head of celery into sticks and remove the leaves. Coarsely chop three of the outside celery stalks and the biggest of the leaves. Keep the inner tender stalks and leaves.

Chop the clove of garlic and the tomato. Peel the onion and cut a $\frac{1}{2}$ cm ($\frac{1}{4}$ inch) slice off the top. Put the boiling water into a saucepan with the coarsely chopped celery, garlic, tomato, the slice of onion and thyme leaves. Season with half a teaspoon of salt and some black pepper. Bring the pan to the boil and simmer for 15–20 minutes while you make the soup.

To make the soup, dice the rest of the onion. Heat the oil and butter in a large saucepan and gently sweat the onion until soft. Slice the rest of the celery into $\frac{1}{2}$ cm ($\frac{1}{4}$ inch) slices across the stalks and add to the onion. Toss to coat with the oil and butter and sweat until the celery is softening. Keep the heat fairly low so as not to let the butter burn.

Strain the stock from the pot and discard the flavourings. Add the roast tomatoes to the celery and onion, making sure you get all the golden gooey stuff from the roasting dish by rinsing it out with some of the strained stock. Add this and the rest of the stock to the saucepan; bring to the boil and simmer until the celery is soft and the tomatoes have broken up.

Purée the soup in a blender or food processor.

vegetable fritters

Serves about 6

We don't often have deep-fried food, but once or twice a summer we do these fritters, or 'battered vegetables', as Tom once found them described on a menu; the same menu contained a salad of 'autumn leaves'.

The batter will keep overnight in the fridge, but is best used on the day it's made. The fritters have to be eaten as soon as they are cooked, so we tend to stand round chatting and eating as they are cooked rather than taking them to the table. They are really good as an informal start to a Sunday buffet lunch.

Batter
100 g (4 oz) flour
pinch of salt
2 small–medium eggs, separated
2 tbsp olive oil
160 ml (5½ fl oz) lager or
   sparkling water

Sift the flour and salt into a bowl. Make a well in the centre and add the egg yolks and oil. Whisk the yolks and oil together and gradually whisk in the flour. When the yolks and oil have absorbed as much flour as they can hold, start adding the lager or sparkling water until you have added it all. Whisk the egg whites and fold them into the batter.

Vegetables

courgettes

aubergines

male flowers from courgettes,
  pumpkin or squashes

peppers

French beans

scallions

parsley leaves

basil

To cook

sunflower or peanut oil

lemon wedges

salt and pepper

Cut the courgettes and aubergines into ¹/₂ cm (¹/₄ inch) thick slices. Male flowers on courgette, pumpkin and squash plants are the ones on a stalk without a baby fruit directly behind the flower. They are best when just opened and there are no brown edges to the petals. Check them for insects.

Cut the peppers into ¹/₂ cm (¹/₄ inch) wide strips. Top and tail the French beans, pulling any strings off as you go. Trim the scallions into 6 cm (2¹/₂ inches) lengths. Wash and dry the parsley if necessary. Take the top 4 leaves of each flowering stem of basil; these are the best part of the plant to use, though any large basil leaves will do.

Pour enough sunflower or peanut oil into a large saucepan or wok to fill it one-third full and heat; alternatively, heat oil in a deep fat fryer to 185°C/365°F. Check the temperature by dropping in a teaspoonful of batter and seeing how quickly it browns – if it browns too fast, turn the heat down a little; if too slow, allow more time to heat up.

Dip the vegetable pieces into the batter and then into the hot oil, 4 or 5 pieces at a time. Do not overcrowd the oil, as this reduces the temperature and they do not cook as quickly. Turn the vegetables over in the oil to cook evenly. Remove when golden and drain on lots of kitchen paper. Eat immediately with a squeeze of lemon and a sprinkle of salt and pepper. After each batch, give the oil a moment or two to heat up again before cooking the next batch.

The French beans and scallion pieces may be cooked singly or in clumps of 3 or 4. The flowers and herbs are particularly delicious cooked this way.

aubergines with pesto

Serves 4 as a starter or light main course

The aubergines can be browned under the grill instead of in the oven. The pesto will keep for a week or so in the fridge if it is kept in jars with a film of oil on top, but it's really best when first made. It goes very well with any form of pasta, spread on crostini or stirred into a tomato-based vegetable soup at the last minute.

Pesto

60 g (2 oz) basil

2 cloves of garlic

60 g (2 oz) pine nuts

60 g (2 oz) parmesan, grated

pinch of salt

extra virgin olive oil

Pound the above ingredients together, except for the oil, in a mortar or whiz in the food processor. Thin the mixture with the olive oil to a thick paste.

4 small aubergines about 12 cm (5 inches) long

salt

olive oil

pesto

parmesan, grated

Set the oven to GM5/190°C/375°F.

Cut the aubergines into 1 cm (½ inch) thick slices lengthways, sprinkle with salt and leave to drain in a colander for 30 minutes. Rinse off the salt and squeeze dry on kitchen paper.

Heat up a heavy frying pan or ridged grill pan on a moderate to high heat. Brush the aubergine slices with oil and brown both sides on the pan. When all the slices are done, lay out flat on a baking tray and smear on a thin layer of pesto and top with a grating of parmesan. Bake in the oven for 15–20 minutes, until browned. Serve with bread to mop up the oil.

tomato salsa

This is really nice with barbecued meats, particularly sausages and hamburgers. We even eat it as a dip with pieces of flatbread. Feel free to leave in the chilli seeds if you want a hotter salsa.

8 tomatoes

8 scallions, chopped

2 green chillies, seeds removed and chopped

juice of 1 lime

3 tbsp fresh coriander, chopped

Bring a kettle of water to the boil and put the tomatoes in a heatproof bowl. When the water is boiling, pour it over the tomatoes and leave for 3 minutes. Pour off the hot water and peel the tomatoes.

Chop the tomatoes and blend with the scallions, chillies and lime juice in a blender or a food processor. Stir in the coriander. Mix together and season with salt and pepper.

bolognese

Serves 4–6

This is our version of the Italian classic ragu from Bologna. We use this sauce with pasta or to make lasagne.

1 large onion

2 cloves of garlic

1 stick of celery

1 small–medium carrot

6 tbsp olive oil

4 streaky rashers

300 g (10 oz) minced beef

150 ml (5 fl oz) white wine

400 g (14 oz) can of chopped tomatoes or 500 g (1 lb 2 oz) very ripe tomatoes, skinned and chopped

150 ml (5 fl oz) milk

bay leaf

salt and pepper

Peel and slice the onion, garlic, celery and carrot as finely as possible. Heat 3 tablespoons of oil in a frying pan over a medium heat and add the chopped vegetables, cooking them slowly until soft, and remove to a plate.

Chop the rashers into small pieces. Pour 3 more spoonfuls of oil into the pan and turn up the heat. Add the rashers and mince to the pan and break the mince up with a fork. Fry the mince and rashers until dry and beginning to brown.

Add the wine, return the vegetables to the pan and add the chopped tomatoes. Bring to the boil and mash the contents of the pan with a potato masher. Add the milk (I know it sounds odd, but it gives a richness to the sauce), stir it in well and add the bay leaf, salt and pepper to taste.

Turn down the heat to a simmer. Simmer for 1 hour, topping up with water if the sauce starts to dry out.

field mushroom sauce

Serves 4

Some years are better mushroom years than others, and once a patch of mushrooms is found we will check it every day during August and into September if the weather holds. Field mushrooms are the wild cousins of the button and open/flat cap mushrooms available in the supermarket. Do not pick wild mushrooms unless you are 110 per cent sure you know what they are. Small packets of dried ceps from France or porcini from Italy are available in delicatessens. We use some of these soaked in boiling water to give extra flavour to shop mushrooms, especially if the wild ones are elusive.

2 large shallots

5 streaky rashers (optional)

2 tbsp olive oil

field mushrooms, cleaned and sliced, about 5 handfuls for 4 people

270–300 ml (9–10 fl oz) cream

50 g (2 oz) parmesan, grated

nutmeg

salt and pepper

300 g (10 oz) pasta

Put a large pan of salted water on to boil for the pasta. Peel and thinly slice the shallots. Cut the rashers into narrow strips. Heat the oil in a frying pan and cook the shallots and rasher pieces until the shallot is soft and the rasher pieces are browning.

Add the mushrooms and turn up the heat. Watch the pan and stir the mushrooms until they are soft and most of the moisture has evaporated. Add the cream to the pan and bring to the boil. Take off the heat and stir in the parmesan. Season with some grated nutmeg, pepper and salt if necessary.

When the water comes to the boil, cook the pasta according to the packet instructions. Drain the pasta well and mix with the sauce.

plums with hazelnut crumble

Serves 4

We have one hazelnut plant which the rabbits have not nibbled to death – yet – and we are waiting patiently for it to produce nuts. In the meantime, we buy them. We also freeze plums to have this dessert out of season; we cut the plums in half and freeze them in 1 litre tubs.

40 g (2 oz) hazelnuts
40 g (2 oz) butter
80 g (3 oz) brown flour
25 g (1 oz) demerara sugar
12 plums

Set the oven to GM6/200°C/400°F.

Coarsely chop the hazelnuts by hand or in a food processor, then toast the hazelnuts in a dry pan until they colour. Leave to cool.

Rub the butter into the flour and stir in the sugar and nuts. Halve the plums and remove the stones. Arrange the plums in an ovenproof dish, cut side up, in a single layer. Sprinkle the crumble mix over the top, leaving the surface rough.

Bake for 20–30 minutes, until the top bits darken. Serve with whipped cream. This is also very good for breakfast with yoghurt.

plum jam

Makes 5–6 jars

When the plums are ripe, we eat them like sweets off the trees – two to three bites and they're gone. Some, though, we will make jam with for scones or morning toast.

1 kg (2 lb) plums
300 ml (10 fl oz) water
1 kg (2 lb) sugar

For hints and tips on jam making, see Seville Orange Marmalade, pp. 26–7.

Cut the plums into quarters and remove the stones. Put the pieces of plum and the water into a large saucepan and bring to the boil. Simmer the plums until they are soft. We put the lid on the pan and into the simmering oven of the Aga for 20–30 minutes.

When the plums are soft, add the sugar and stir until dissolved. Turn up the heat and bring to the boil. Put a small plate into the fridge and 6 jars to sterilise in a low oven at GM1/140°C/285°F. Boil the jam for 10 minutes and check for the setting point (see pp. 26–7). Test for setting by putting a teaspoonful of the jam onto the cold plate in the fridge and letting it cool. If the top of the jam wrinkles when pushed, the jam is ready, otherwise boil the jam for another 5 minutes and try again.

When the jam is ready, take it off the heat and let it cool. After 10 minutes, take the jars out of the oven and pour in the hot jam and seal. Leave to cool and label.

september

garden

September is often a very summery month, but the evenings are drawing in now, and it's important to remember that most vegetables need not just reasonably mild conditions, but also quite a lot of daylight. Many gardeners think they can sow stuff on warm, sunny September days, but while they will germinate and even survive in some form, the lack of light means that they will not grow.

There are exceptions, of course, and we continue to sow salad crops in the polytunnel. The main task in September, however, is to see that the plants that will deliver during the autumn and the winter are well fed, free of pests and, if need be, properly staked against the coming winds. If we manage to get the ground clear of weeds at this stage, it's likely to remain fairly clean until spring, at which point digging will be much easier.

September sees the first of the pears and the quinces. Pears are trickier than apples by and large, because they flower earlier and are more prone to being decimated by frost. But few things compare to eating a perfect pear from your own tree – except, of course, that most of them cannot be eaten straight from the branch. Generally speaking, pears need to be harvested on the brink of ripeness and allowed to finish off, so to speak, for a week or so indoors. Knowing the point at which to pick is a matter of experience and we have not quite perfected it yet. Most will ripen to a luscious, sweet juiciness, but some will remain as hard as hell and end up in the compost bucket.

Quinces are different. They are meant to stay hard and they need a lot of cooking. Sliced thinly and incorporated into an apple pie, they add a very distinctive flavour and can smell so strong that one or two of them will perfume a whole room. Almost by definition, they are the kind of thing that you have to grow yourself, rather like medlars.

There are times that we curse the brambles. So prolific are they that every spring we have to get the margins of our fields cut back by a very big and noisy piece of agri-equipment. Otherwise, they would meet in the middle and take over.

But in September we get a crop of blackberries so huge that we can afford to let the birds take most of it. A perfectly ripe blackberry, plucked in a dry September, produces one of the most magical flavours known to humanity. The French know this very well and produce *crème de mures* from such fruit. If you swirl a quarter of a teaspoon of this liqueur into a glass of champagne, you get an ethereal version of the real thing.

It depends on the year, of course, but generally the field mushrooms start to appear in our paddock as August merges with September and they will continue to pop up, almost overnight, well into October. It's not a coincidence that this only started to happen after we had brought the land back into essentially organic production. Concentrated chemical fertilizers seem to inhibit field mushrooms, but a fairly large mycelium seems to have survived below ground.

Nothing, not even a cep or a chanterelle, is quite as good as your own field mushroom (*agaricus campestris*) grilled with a bit of butter for breakfast. We also get a few parasols and the odd shaggy ink cap and the kind of boletus that is closely related to ceps but tends to go a bit slimy when cooked. The trick here is to use them in a risotto.

In the woods of west Waterford we pick common chanterelles in their thousands, but you have to know where to look and what you're looking for. The chances of being fatally poisoned are higher than many people think. Some foolish folk have confused the field mushroom for something not entirely dissimilar, called the Death Cap. Enough said.

recipes

September arrives and the girls go back to school, a new year and new challenges. The polytunnel and garden are still in full production and preserving will have to fit in round school runs and after-school activities.

Sweetcorn is ready at the beginning of September. We put the pot of water on to boil before picking the cobs and then they only need 5–7 minutes in the boiling water. Sometimes we cut the kernels off the cobs to cook in a pot with a knob of butter, over a low heat, and swirl in a couple of tablespoons of cream at the end to make creamed corn.

Blackberries line the hedges and the first of the apples are ready. Elderberries will be ripening and ready for picking. The first of the squashes and pumpkins make a welcome return. There are still raspberries to be picked too.

french onion soup

Serves 4

When making chicken stock for onion soup, add any loose onion skins that happen to be in the vegetable basket to give the stock a good strong colour. Use a well-flavoured hard cheese for the topping, such as Hegarty's cheddar or Desmond.

3–4 onions, about 450 g (1 lb)

3 tbsp olive oil

1 small glass of white wine or medium sherry

1 litre (1¾ pints) stock

salt and pepper

8 thin slices of French bread

110 g (4 oz) cheese, grated

Peel and thinly slice the onions into rings. Heat the oil in a wide pot over a medium heat to simmer, then add the sliced onions. Turn the onions in the oil and turn up the heat. Keep stirring the onions until they begin to colour and soften.

Add the wine and let the alcohol evaporate. Turn down the heat and let the onions stew until soft. They need to caramelise and produce a golden brown goo on the bottom of the pot, but be careful not to let them burn.

Add the stock and seasoning and bring to the boil. Turn down the heat and let the pot simmer while you make the cheese on toast. Grill the bread on one side only and turn over. Put the grated cheese on the untoasted side and put back under the hot grill until it bubbles. Put 2 pieces of the toasted cheese into each bowl and ladle over the soup.

crostini

bread

Good yeast bread or the potato bread from the February chapter (see pp. 42–3) is what we use for crostini. All the better if the bread is a day old, as it toasts really well.

Pizza dough (see pp. 17–18) also makes a good loaf of bread. After it has risen in the bowl, gently knead and shape it into one round loaf, or cut in half and make two smaller, longer loaves. Place on a greased baking sheet and dust with flour. Leave to rise again for 20–30 minutes. Make some slashes with a sharp knife on the top of the bread and leave to rise for another 10–15 minutes. Bake in a hot oven at GM7/220°C/425°F for 20–40 minutes for the big loaf or 20–30 minutes for the two smaller ones. They are done when they sound hollow when tapped underneath.

Toppings

tomatoes

scallions

parsley

courgettes

roast tomatoes

basil leaves

pesto

tapenade

olive oil, garlic pepper and salt

garlic

your best olive oil

Skin and chop some tomatoes, finely chop a few scallions and some parsley, mix together with a pinch of salt, pepper and a dollop or two of olive oil.

To grill the courgettes, cut lengthways into $\frac{1}{2}$ cm ($\frac{1}{4}$ inch) thick slices, brush with oil and cook on a hot ridged grill pan or on a heavy frying pan.

Cut the bread into 1 cm ($\frac{1}{2}$ inch) thick slices and toast. If you have a ridged grill pan, use that, as it gives the toast nice dark lines. Rub each slice with a skinned clove of garlic – the toast acts like sandpaper and wears away the garlic onto it. How much garlic you rub on is a matter of preference.

Put the toasts garlic side up on a serving platter and top with the above toppings. Don't pile too high if they are to be finger food handed round with drinks – two bites each is best.

aubergine parmigiano

Serves 4

This is glut food. By now the polytunnel is dripping with tomatoes and aubergines. Having a batch of tomato sauce bubbling away in the simmering oven, while we slice and cook the aubergines, feels good.

We normally make a double amount and line the second dish with cling film and freeze it instead of baking it in the oven. Using the cling film means we can take it out of the dish after it has been frozen. When we want to use it, we take the cling film-wrapped block out of the freezer, unwrap it and put it into the dish it was originally frozen in, and leave it to defrost before baking it in a hot oven.

A can or two of chopped tomatoes can be used instead of fresh ones. As fresh tomatoes vary in their water content, 1 kg (2 lb) is an approximate amount. If you have more, cook them up; you can always freeze the extra.

1 kg (2 lb) fresh tomatoes

2 onions

3 tbsp olive oil

3 cloves of garlic

salt and pepper

2–3 aubergines

250 g (9 oz) mozzarella cheese

basil leaves

30 g (1 oz) parmesan, grated

Put the tomatoes into a large bowl and pour over boiling water. Leave for 2–3 minutes, pour off the water and skin the tomatoes. Peel and slice the onions.

Heat the olive oil in a frying pan and add the onions. Cook until soft. Peel the garlic and finely grate it into the onions. Roughly chop the tomatoes and add to the onions and garlic in the frying pan. Season with salt and pepper and bring to the boil. Simmer until the sauce is fairly thick. Mash with a potato masher to break up any large chunks of tomato.

While the tomato is cooking, slice the aubergines into $1/2$ cm ($1/4$ inch) thick slices and brush with oil. Heat a heavy frying pan or ridged grill pan and cook the aubergine slices on both sides until browned.

Cut the mozzarella into thin-ish slices (about the same size as the aubergine slices). Take the leaves off the basil stalks.

Set the oven to GM5/190°C/375°F. Oil an ovenproof dish and put in about a third of the tomato sauce, followed by a layer of aubergine and a layer of mozzarella and some basil leaves. Repeat with another third of the tomato sauce, the rest of the aubergine, then the mozzarella and basil. Top with the last third of the tomato sauce. Sprinkle with grated parmesan and bake in the oven for about 35 minutes, until bubbling and browned. Great with salad and crusty bread.

aubergine and yoghurt purée

Serves 6

Aubergines do well in the tunnel and are particularly good grilled on the barbecue. We eat this purée with flatbreads or raw vegetables as a starter or pre-dinner nibble. It's also good as a sauce for barbecued meat.

1 large aubergine
1 tsp coriander seeds
1 clove of garlic
juice of ½ lemon
300 g (10 oz) tub of thick natural yoghurt
salt and pepper
fresh coriander, chopped
pitta bread

Grill the aubergine until the skin is blackened, or roast in the oven until soft. Using the oven means you lose some of the smoky flavour and the time it takes depends on the size of the aubergine.

Toast the coriander seeds in a dry pan until they change colour slightly. Take off the heat, cool and grind to a powder.

Scrape the skin off the aubergine and chop the flesh. Put the aubergine flesh, garlic and ground coriander into a food processor or blender. Add a good squeeze of lemon juice and enough yoghurt to make a thick purée.

Season with more lemon, salt and pepper. Sprinkle with fresh coriander and serve with pittas or flatbreads.

smoked haddock supper

Serves 4–6 with other food

Good fish is a scarce thing and is becoming scarcer. When we can get real smoked haddock (not the white fish coated in luminous orange stuff), we make this supper dish. Real smoked haddock still has its skin on and the flesh is a creamy tan colour where it has been in contact with real smoke. Sometimes we share out the haddock, etc. between 4–6 ramekins and serve as a starter. They will cook in a shorter time, so check after 10–15 minutes.

500 g (1 lb 2 oz) piece of smoked haddock

6 ripe tomatoes

12 scallions

butter

300 ml (10 fl oz) cream

pepper

100 g (4 oz) breadcrumbs

3 tbsp parsley, chopped

Set the oven to GM6/200°C/400°F.

Put the haddock into a heatproof dish and cover with boiling water. Cut the tomatoes into eighths and remove the green cores. Finely chop the scallions.

Drain the haddock and remove the flesh from the skin and bones. Butter a shallow ovenproof dish. Put the haddock, tomatoes and scallions into the dish and gently mix so that the fish and scallions are evenly distributed amongst the tomatoes. Pour the cream over everything and season with pepper.

Mix the breadcrumbs and parsley and spread over the top of the fish and tomatoes. Dot the top with a few pieces of butter and bake in the oven for about 30 minutes, until bubbling and browned on top. If the top browns before the centre is hot, cover the top loosely with a butter paper or foil.

Serve with a green salad and some sautéed courgettes.

lamb arm stew

Serves 6

This stew got its name after a discussion in the butcher's about how many legs a sheep has. 'Two!' declared the butcher. 'Four when it's alive and two when it's dead,' claimed his assistant. So what were the other two legs called when the sheep was dead? 'Arms,' we concluded. The 'arms' are the bony bits that stick out of the shoulder of lamb. They are best slow cooked and give the sauce an almost sticky texture from the meat fibres and connective tissue breaking down.

4 tbsp olive oil

6 lamb arms/fore shanks

2 onions

3 cloves of garlic

1 kg (2 lb) tomatoes

6 stalks of celery

3 peppers

3 carrots

3 sprigs of thyme

1 bay leaf

salt and pepper

Set the oven to GM3/170°C/340°F.

Heat the oil in a casserole and brown the arms/shanks. Remove and turn the heat to low. Peel and slice the onions and garlic. Add to the casserole and cook until soft.

While the onions are softening, skin the tomatoes by covering with boiling water for 2 minutes and draining them. The skins will then peel off easily. Chop the tomatoes and remove the green core.

Wash the celery and cut it into 1 cm ($^1/_2$ inch) slices. Cut the peppers into 2 cm ($^3/_4$ inch) wide strips and the carrots into 1 cm ($^1/_2$ inch) wide slices.

Return the meat to the casserole and add the chopped vegetables, thyme and bay leaf. Season with salt and pepper and bring to the boil.

Put the lid on the casserole and pop it in the oven for about 1 hour and 45 minutes. The meat should fall off the bones when it's done.

onion and goat's cheese pizza

Makes 4 pizzas

Anchovies aren't a great favourite in our house, so *pissaladiere*, with its lattice of anchovies, wasn't going to be a runner; though the onion made a good topping for pizza, it needed something tangy. We tried some feta and liked the result. Later we discovered Jane Murphy's Ardsallagh goat's cheese and started to use that. The classic herb for onions is sage, so we added some and our favourite pizza was born.

1 level tsp dried yeast
¼ tsp sugar
280 ml (10 fl oz) hand-hot water
1 tsp salt
430 g (1 lb) strong white flour
oil
4 large onions
1 tub of soft goat's cheese – we
  like Ardsallagh (120 g/4½ oz for
  4 pizzas)
10 sage leaves

Mix the yeast, sugar and some of the warm water in a cup and leave in a warm place to froth. Add the salt to the rest of the warm water and keep warm. Weigh the flour and sieve it into a bowl (warm the bowl first if your house is on the cool side).

The yeast is ready when it has a head like a pint of stout. Pour the yeast into the flour and rinse out the cup with some of the warm water, then pour into the flour, adding the rest of the water. Flours vary in the amount of water they need; you may need more or less than the amount given.

Mix the water in and start to knead the dough, either in a mixer with a dough hook or by hand. Keep kneading until the dough is smooth and springy. Take the dough out of the bowl and pour a tablespoon of oil into the bowl. Put the dough back into the bowl and smear it with oil. Cover the bowl and leave to rise. The time taken to rise depends on temperature – 60 to 90 minutes somewhere warm or all day somewhere cooler.

While the dough is rising, peel, halve and thinly slice the onions. Heat the olive oil in a heavy frying pan and cook the onions slowly over a low heat until soft and golden. Take the pan off the heat and leave to cool.

When the dough has doubled in size and has a domed top, it's ready to use.

Switch the oven to its highest setting and put a flat baking sheet onto the rack in the hottest part of the oven. Divide the dough into 4 balls, dust with flour and set aside. It needs a rest before shaping.

Put the sage leaves on top of each other and slice into narrow strips across the leaves.

Take a ball of dough and gently squeeze and stretch it out into a circle about 26 cm (10 inches) in diameter. Put the dough onto a floured, flat baking sheet and cover the centre with a layer of onion, leaving a 1 cm ($^1/_2$ inch) edge.

Dot with spoonfuls of goat's cheese and sprinkle with the sage leaves, salt, pepper and a dribble of olive oil.

Shake the baking sheet gently to get the pizza to move, then slide the pizza onto the sheet in the oven. Close the oven door and make up the next pizza, by which time the first pizza will be almost ready. It may need to be turned for even cooking. Slide out the cooked pizza on a long fish slice onto a plate and slide in the next pizza. Keep going, sharing the pizzas as they come out of the oven.

blackberry and apple pie

Serves 6–8

Autumn is blackberries and apples; almost free food at this time of year. The proportion of apples to blackberries is as variable as how many blackberries you can pick and get home to be cooked. Sometimes there may only be purple smears left in the collection containers and on happy hands and faces. When this happens, don't despair, everyone loves apple pie! The sweetness of apples varies and you may feel that this pie needs more sugar; we like ours quite tart.

Flaky pastry
250 g (9 oz) plain flour
185 g (6 oz) very cold butter
150–160 ml (5 fl oz) cold water

Sift the flour into a bowl. Cut the butter into small cubes about 1 cm (½ inch) square and stir gently into the flour. Pour in the cold water and mix to a stiff dough with a knife. Shape into a rough rectangle. Wrap and leave to cool in the fridge for 30 minutes.

Remove from the fridge and place on a floured surface. Roll out into a 1 cm (½ inch) thick rectangle with a floured rolling pin. Fold the pastry in three and turn so that the three layers are towards you and roll out again, then fold in three again, turn, roll and fold again. Wrap and leave in the fridge for 1 hour.

Filling

500–600 g (1 lb 4 oz) cooking apples

300 g (10 oz) blackberries

40 g (1½ oz) sugar

Set the oven to GM6/200°C/400°F.

Peel the apples, cut into quarters and remove the cores. Thinly slice the apples and mix with the blackberries and sugar.

Cut the pastry in half and roll out one half to cover a 26 cm (10 inch) pie plate. Line the plate with pastry and trim the edges. Roll out the other half so that it's slightly larger than the plate. This is for the top of the pie.

Put the apples and blackberries onto the pastry on the plate, leaving a 1 cm (½ inch) strip around the edge. Brush the edge of the pastry with milk or beaten egg.

Lay the other piece of pastry on top of the pie and carefully cut the extra pastry away from the edge of the plate. Squeeze the edges of the pastry together. Make a small hole in the top of the pie with a knife and paint the top of the pie with milk or a beaten egg.

Bake in the hot oven for 20 minutes. Leave to cool for a while before serving.

raspberry jam

Makes about 4–5 jars

We do not go in for marathon jam-making sessions, so cooking up a few tubs of raspberries from the garden or freezer when there's time to spare may not be as efficient, but it's quicker. If using frozen fruit, weigh the tub of berries without its lid, put the berries into the pot and then weigh the same weight of sugar into the tub as there were raspberries. Keep the tubs of sugar beside the cooker for when needed.

1 kg (2 lb) raspberries
1 kg (2 lb) sugar
a knob of butter or a tablespoon
   of sunflower oil
5 clean jars

For hints and tips on jam making, see Seville Orange Marmalade, pp. 26–7.

Place a saucer in the fridge to chill. Put the raspberries into a large pot and place on a low heat. As the juice starts to run, turn up the heat. When there's lots of juice, bring the pot to the boil and cook until the fruit is soft and breaking up.

Turn down the heat halfway and add the sugar. Stir in the sugar until it's all dissolved. Turn up the heat and bring back to the boil. While the jam is boiling, turn the oven to GM1/140°C/285°F and put 5 clean jars in to sterilise.

Boil the jam for 15 minutes and test for setting by putting a teaspoonful of the hot jam onto the cold saucer in the fridge. Turn down the heat under the pot while the test cools in the fridge. The setting point has been reached when the jam wrinkles when pushed from the edge. If the tester doesn't do this after a few minutes, boil the jam for another 5 minutes and try again.

When the jam is ready, add a knob of butter or a tablespoon of sunflower oil to disperse the foam and take off the heat. Let the jam cool for 15 minutes and then pot into the hot jars and seal.

elderberry chutney

Makes 2–3 jars

Once the elderberries start to hang down, they are ripening, and autumn is well and truly on its way. On a dry day, walking the hedges and woods looking for these inky black berries is an enjoyable form of exercise. You need quite a large basket for this amount, but it's worth it. Pick whole heads of berries and when you get home, comb the berries from the stalks into a large bowl using a fork.

700 g (1 lb 8 oz) elderberries, removed from their stalks
300 ml (10 fl oz) vinegar
100 g (4 oz) onions
100 g (4 oz) sultanas
100 g (4 oz) sugar
1 level tsp salt
1 cm fresh ginger, grated
1 level tsp ground cinnamon
5 green cardamom pods, lightly crushed

For hints and tips on chutney making, see Seville Orange Marmalade, pp. 26–7.

Heat the berries with the vinegar in a stainless steel or enamel pot. Finely slice the onion and when the berries come to the boil, add to the pot. Add all the other ingredients and simmer until thick.

Pour into hot sterilised jars and cover. Wipe the mouth of the jars clean, as the vinegar will react with metal lids, or use plastic lids instead.

october

garden

By the middle of October, the celeriac which earlier in the year sulked and refused to grow will have reached maturity. On the few occasions that we see celeriac in the supermarket, this rather knobbly root vegetable is the size of a small swede. I have no idea how it can be grown to these proportions, at least in Ireland at any rate. Our ones, usually the variety known as Prinz, which is slow to bolt, are the size of a cricket ball and they are tender and delicious in a strong celery-flavoured way.

Fergus Henderson of London's remarkable St John restaurant mixes grated celeriac and salt in roughly equal measures and lets it sit in the fridge for a few days. Then he dries it out in a slow oven before grinding it up to produce his version of celery salt. This old-fashioned condiment is great with hardboiled eggs of all varieties.

We like to leave our celeriac in the ground until it is needed because this keeps it perfectly fresh. Of course, if you have a slug problem this approach may leave you with celeriac that is, as they say, holier than godly. The roots can be lifted and stored in a cool place in boxes of dry sand or earth.

Slugs are less likely to munch their way through parsnips, another vegetable that reaches maturity in October. The problem with parsnips is that they taste rather bland and floury at this point in the year. As for the many people who utterly detest parsnips, this is the least of the root's problems.

However, when parsnips have been exposed to a few hard frosts – which are becoming rarer as this planet of ours warms up – the starch is converted to sugar and this very humble vegetable becomes sweeter and much more attractive, so we tend to leave ours to the weather until Christmas at the earliest.

Caterpillar squashing continues through October on all of the cabbage tribe, not least the cavolo nero, or Tuscan cabbage, which comes into its own as autumn turns into winter. The long, narrow, bubbly and dark green leaves tend to furl, thus concealing the odd caterpillar. Very careful attention is called for when preparing cavolo nero for cooking, otherwise you might get more protein than you bargained for – and caterpillars taste quite bitter when cooked!

Our particular collection of apples is ready for harvest in October. First come the juicy little Katies, which are crunchy and sweet, but they don't keep. We pick and eat them straight away as we wait for the others to reach perfection.

The Cox's Orange Pippins (if you have an old apple tree in the garden, it's almost certainly one of these) are supposed to be the greatest dessert apple of them all and there's no doubt that, at its best, it's magnificent. Good Cox's are like the great Riesling Kabinett wines of the Mosel, sweet but with breathtaking acidity. We tend to eat ours after dinner, with a chunk of Dan Hegarty's remarkable farmhouse cheddar which is made near Cork city and is right up there with the ideal Somerset cheddars like Keene's and Quicke's.

The Cox's close relation, Worcester Pearmain, is another superb apple: generally a bit bigger, a little sweeter and perhaps less austere on the palate. For us, they seem to ripen about a fortnight ahead of their more famous cousins.

Last to ripen are the great old Bramley Seedlings, everyone's favourite cooking apple. They get so big and heavy (some of them come close to a kilo) that the limbs of our young trees are weighed down to the ground and we have to be quick to save the apples from the rabbits and the rats.

Our Cox's can be kept for a month to six weeks in the cool larder before they go wrinkly on the outside and a bit dry within. The Bramleys, on the other hand, will carry on until the early spring if we choose perfect specimens, wrap each one in newspaper and store them in one of the old outbuildings (mice permitting).

We usually pick our last cucumber in late October (when it often smells bizarrely of melon at this late stage) and the tomatoes struggle on until the end of the month. As November dawns, everything is looking rather tattered.

recipes

October is when we begin to prepare for winter. The polytunnel needs to be cleared out and the last of the cucumbers, tomatoes and aubergines used up. Seasonality is wonderful: in May we were anticipating the first cucumber and tomato, by October we have eaten our fill and are looking forward to the winter vegetables. Variety is the spice of life.

celeriac soup

Serves 4

This ugly root is a first cousin of celery. It has celery's flavour without the strings and makes an off-white, creamy soup.

1 celeriac, about 350–400 g
   (12–14 oz) – 300 g (10 oz) in
   peeled weight
1 large onion
3 tbsp oil and a knob of butter
750 ml (1 pint 5 fl oz) stock
salt and pepper
180 ml (6 fl oz) cream

Peel the celeriac and cut the flesh into small cubes. Peel and slice the onion. Heat the oil and butter in a large saucepan. Add the onion and cook on a low heat until the onion is soft. Add the celeriac cubes to the onion and stir to coat with the oil. Pour half the stock into the celeriac and onion and bring to the boil. Put the lid on and simmer until the celeriac is soft.

Take off the heat and leave to cool before you purée the contents of the saucepan using a hand-held blender or a food processor. (If time is limited, add some of the reserved cold stock and purée right away.) Add the rest of the stock and reheat the soup. Taste and season. Lightly whip the cream and fold into the hot soup just before serving.

pumpkin filo pastry parcels

Makes about 36

We aren't sure whether these should be sweet or savoury or perhaps in between in a Middle Eastern style. Add some slowly cooked caramelised onion for a savoury version. Pumpkins vary in their sweetness and the longer they are stored, the sweeter they become. We have not yet mastered filo pastry, so we buy it frozen.

1 pumpkin, about 750 g (1 lb 10 oz) or 430 g (15 oz) cooked mashed pumpkin
½ tsp cinnamon
sugar to taste
270 g (10 oz) packet of filo pastry
melted butter or oil
icing sugar

Heat the oven to GM6/200°C/400°F.

Cut the pumpkin into 8 wedges and remove the seeds. Put the pumpkin on a baking tray and bake for 20 minutes. Take out of the oven and leave to cool for 5 minutes. Scoop the cooked pumpkin flesh off the skins and mash with cinnamon. Taste and add sugar if you like.

Unwrap the filo pastry and cut in 7 cm (3 inch) squares. Brush each square with butter or oil. Line bun tins with 3 oiled squares of filo. Fill with a teaspoon of pumpkin and fold over the corners. Bake for 12 minutes. Remove from the tray and cool on a wire rack. Dust with icing sugar and a little ground cinnamon. Serve warm.

gem store squashes with tarragon cream

French tarragon won't survive outdoors over winter. It needs protection, so we grow it in the tunnel. Before we had a tunnel we grew it in a pot and brought it inside in the winter.

Roast chicken with tarragon is a classic regular roast dinner here, so when there was some tarragon-y gravy left over one day, we reheated it and poured it into some baked half squashes as a lunch. Eaten with a spoon, it made a real comfort dish. As gravy is not always available, we tried this version without it.

Per person

½ squash

6 cm (3 inch) sprig of tarragon

knob of butter

salt and pepper

3 tbsp cream

Heat the oven to GM5/190°C/375°F.

Scoop the seeds out of the centre of the squash. Strip the leaves from the tarragon and place in the hole where the seeds were, along with the knob of butter. Sprinkle with salt and pepper and put into the oven and bake for 30 minutes. They should be soft enough to eat with a spoon. Pour in the cream and pop back into the oven for 5 minutes for the cream to heat through.

waldorf salad

Serves 4

There are three essential ingredients for Waldorf salad, and all are at their best in October: apples, celery and walnuts. We were lucky to have four established apple trees in the garden when we moved here. The blossoms are a joy in the spring and the apples a boon for the autumn.

Celery grows well outside in the vegetable garden and will stand until the really bad frosts come.

Having planted three walnut trees, we are waiting patiently for them to fruit. In the meantime, we take advantage of the Hallowe'en nuts and buy a few extra bags of walnuts to add to this salad.

2 dessert apples
2 tbsp lemon juice
4 celery sticks
10 walnuts in their shells
3–4 tbsp mayonnaise
salt and pepper

Cut the apples into 2½ cm (1 inch) pieces and toss in the lemon juice. Cut the celery into 2 cm (¾ inch) slices and add to the apples. Shell the walnuts and break the nuts into pieces, then add to the apple and celery. Stir in the mayonnaise and taste. Season if necessary.

hake with stewed peppers

Serves 4

Any white fish is good with these peppers and all you need is some salad and perhaps some mashed potato or bread to mop up the peppers' juice. Any leftover peppers are good as a topping for crostini.

1 onion
2 cloves of garlic
2–3 peppers, different colours
your best olive oil
4 fillets of hake
1 tbsp plain flour
salt and pepper

Peel the onion and garlic. Halve and cut it into very thin slices. Cut the top and bottoms off the peppers, then cut them in half lengthways and remove the seeds and core. Cut the flesh of the peppers into long, thin strips.

Put a heavy frying pan on a low heat and pour in about 3–4 tablespoons of olive oil. Let it warm up a bit, then add the onions and garlic. Stir and when they are well coated with oil, add the pepper strips. Turn up the heat until everything starts to sizzle, then turn it back down to low and let the peppers cook very slowly for 30 minutes. When they are soft, remove from the pan and keep warm.

Put the pan over a moderate heat and add 3 more tablespoons of oil. Toss the fillets of hake in the flour mixed with a pinch of salt and a sprinkling of pepper. When the oil is hot, gently lay the hake fillets into the oil, skin side up. Cook until golden, then turn each one over and cook until the other side is golden brown. You may need to turn the heat up slightly to crisp the skin side. Place a fillet each onto hot plates and top with the peppers.

roast beef, roast spuds and horseradish sauce

Beef on the bone serves 5 with leftovers, about 8 boneless

Roast beef is unthinkable without Yorkshire pudding, horseradish sauce and roast potatoes. Yes, Yorkshire puddings are full of refined carbohydrate and fat; traditionally they were eaten as a first course with the gravy to blunt the appetite and make the roast go further. Sometimes they were eaten at the end of the meal with jam and cream if people were still hungry.

Horseradish does interfere with wine, but we like it. We use a mini processor to chop up the horseradish, though be careful when you take off the lid, as the fumes are very strong and will clear the worst blocked nose or sinuses in moments when inhaled.

Kerr's Pinks, Golden Wonders or Roosters make the best roast potatoes around here, and we like about two pieces of roast potato each. The dimensions given are approximate for the potatoes, and if we're running late, we cut them smaller. A lot of our cooking is by feel and from experience.

The beef is the most important part and we like ours well hung and on the bone, which can make carving a little difficult. The crusty bits on the cooked bones are a bonus and after the family has done their best with them, the dog gets to finish them off, so everyone is happy.

A boned and rolled roast is easier to cook rare and there is little or no waste. To get the perfectly roasted piece of beef takes practice and knowing your oven. Also, timing is a major factor – if guests turn up late or early, it can mean the difference between very well done meat or far too many pre-dinner drinks and nibbles. If the meat is ready, it will hold in a warm place covered in foil and a tea towel or two for 15–20 minutes.

2.8 kg (6 lb) roast of beef

Preheat the oven to GM8/230°C/450°F and make sure it's hot. Try to have the meat at room temperature or at least not straight out of the fridge.

Put the meat into a roasting tin and sprinkle with a little salt (particularly on the fat) and pepper. Our butcher gives us some suet to protect the top of the roast, but a smear of oil or a butter paper will do the trick too. Put the roast into the oven. Give it 10–15 minutes to get really hot again and then turn the oven to GM6/200°C/400°F and cook for about 2 hours.

After an hour, remove the fat or covering and add some water to the roasting tin to help with the gravy. (If you are very exacting, invest in a meat thermometer and use it to test the internal heat of the roast. We likes ours at about 65°C/150°F.) The roast should be medium rare after 2 hours. Take it out and let it rest in a warm place while you make the gravy.

Add some hot water to the roasting tin on a low heat and scrape up the dark gungy bits from the bottom of the tin, avoiding the really black bits. In a small saucepan, mix a scant teaspoon of arrowroot or corn flour with some cold water. Strain the gravy from the tin into the saucepan with the water and thickener. Place on the heat and bring to the boil. Let it boil for a minute or two to thicken and skim off the fat. Taste and season if necessary and pour into a gravy boat.

When we are cooking the Yorkshire puds and roast spuds with the roast, we do them in the hottest part of the oven and turn it up to GM7/220°C/425°F for the last 10 minutes of its cooking time. Heat the fat for the Yorkshire puds before you take the meat out to rest and put them in as the meat comes out, leaving the roast spuds in for a final crisping.

197

Roast potatoes

1–2 potatoes per person

olive oil/beef fat

Peel the potatoes and cut into even-sized pieces about 6 cm (2 inches) big, or if they aren't too big, leave them whole. Put the prepared potatoes into the top of a steamer and steam for 5–10 minutes. The outsides should be fluffy but the insides still firm.

Put the potatoes into a roasting tin and coat with oil or melted fat. Any that haven't fluffed up on the outside can be scratched with a fork to roughen their outsides. Roast for 90 minutes at GM7/220°C/425°F. Pop in the oven when you take the fat off the beef.

Horseradish sauce

3 tbsp horseradish, grated

1 tbsp lemon juice

½ tsp mustard powder

100 ml (3½ fl oz) cream, lightly whipped

Put the horseradish into a bowl and add the lemon juice and mustard powder. Mix well to get rid of any lumps of mustard and fold in the cream.

yorkshire pudding

Serves 6

100 g (4 oz) plain flour
1 egg
250 ml (9 fl oz) milk
1 tsp soy sauce

Sift the flour into a bowl and then crack the egg into the flour. Gently mix the egg into some of the flour with a whisk. As the flour and egg thicken, add the milk a splash at a time. Incorporate more and more flour and milk until all the milk is used up. Stir in the soy sauce and pour the batter into a jug.

Preheat the oven to GM7/220°C/425°F.

Put half a teaspoonful of beef fat or oil into each hollow of a 12-cup bun tray. Heat in the oven for 5 minutes. Pour the batter into the hot fat in the hollows to almost fill them. Bake in the hot oven for 25–30 minutes, until they are puffed up and browned.

shepherd's pie

Serves about 4

The great joy of a roast of beef is not just eating it hot with all its accompaniments, but having cold rare meat for salads and sandwiches the next day. The day after, though, is different – the wreck of the roast looks back at you from the larder and pleads to be put out of its misery. It's time for shepherd's pie.

2 onions

2 sticks of celery

1 carrot

2 tbsp oil

700 g (1 lb 8 oz) cold roast beef, minced

gravy mixed with white wine or water to make 300 ml (10 fl oz)

1 heaped tsp tomato purée

1 tbsp Worcestershire sauce

1 tsp mustard powder

sprig of thyme and a bay leaf

salt and pepper

1 kg (2 lb) potatoes

250 ml (9 fl oz) milk

30 g (1 oz) butter

150 g (5 oz) cheddar

Peel and slice the onions and finely dice the celery and carrot. Heat the oil in a frying pan over a moderate heat and add the onion, celery and carrot. Coat the vegetables with oil and cook until soft, then add the minced beef and turn up the heat. Stir the meat and vegetables round until the mix is dry and begins to brown. When there is a thin layer of brown over the bottom of the pan, add the gravy and water or wine. Use this to dissolve any of the brown bits stuck to the bottom of the frying pan.

Stir in the tomato purée, Worcestershire sauce and mustard powder. Pop in the thyme and bay leaf and season with salt and pepper. Bring the pan to the boil and turn down the heat to a simmer. Cook for 30 minutes while you prepare the mashed potatoes. We pop ours into the simmering oven.

Peel and cook the potatoes until soft, then drain. Heat the milk to boiling point. Add the butter to the potatoes and mash. Beat in the hot milk and cheese to the potatoes.

Set the oven to GM6/200°C/400°F. Put the meat mixture into an ovenproof dish and cover with dollops of the mashed potato. Using a fork, roughen the surface of the potato and bake in the hot oven for 20–30 minutes, until browned on top. Peas and tomato ketchup are essential accompaniments.

christmas mincemeat

Getting ready for Christmas happens earlier and earlier each year, and though October may seem a little too early, the tart cooking apples are now at their best for making this.

We really feel we should rename this mix of fruits and spices, as it contains no meat or suet, nor do we put it through a mincer. But everyone thinks of this as Christmas mincemeat for mince pies.

grated zest and juice of 1 lemon
450 g (1 lb) cooking apples, grated
150 g (5 oz) raisins
150 g (5 oz) sultanas
150 g (5 oz) currants
200 g (7 oz) muscovado sugar
100 g (4 oz) dried apricots
 (stoneless)
100 g (4 oz) mixed candied peel
1 cm ($1/2$ inch) fresh ginger
$1/2$ tsp green cardamom seeds
$1/2$ tsp ground cinnamon
$1/2$ tsp ground coriander
$1/4$ tsp nutmeg, grated
40 g (1 $1/2$ oz) butter
60 ml (2 fl oz) whiskey

Put the lemon zest, juice, apples, raisins, sultanas, currants and sugar into a large bowl. Chop the apricots and candied peel into small dice, then add to the bowl. Peel the ginger and grate it into the mix. Roughly crush the cardamom seeds in a mortar and add to the bowl, along with the cinnamon, coriander and nutmeg. Mix well and leave to stand overnight.

The next day, transfer the mixture to a saucepan, bring to the boil and simmer for 10 minutes, until thick. Leave to cool for 10–15 minutes, then stir in the butter and whiskey. Transfer into hot sterilised jars (see pp. 26–7) and seal. This mixture fills a 1 litre preserving jar and we keep it in the back of the fridge.

beetroot cake

When Sarah was in Sixth Class, they made this for a Hallowe'en cookery lesson. It was warily tasted and made a big impression. It makes a good blood-and-guts cake. You can always replace the beetroot with carrot for a less striking effect.

2 eggs

60 ml (2 fl oz) sunflower oil

50 g (2 oz) dark muscovado sugar

150 g (5 oz) brown flour

1 tsp baking powder

100 g (4 oz) beetroot, grated

60 g (2 oz) sultanas

60 g (2 oz) walnuts

Set the oven to GM4/180°C/350°F and line a loaf tin with a butter paper or baking parchment. In a bowl, beat together the eggs, oil and sugar until smooth. Sift in the flour and baking powder and gently mix into the egg mixture. Stir in the beetroot, sultanas and walnuts. Spoon into the prepared tin and bake for 25 minutes or until a skewer comes out clean when poked in.

blackberry and apple jam

Makes approx. 5 pots

The weather is now cool enough for us to consider having a jam session. After the first frosts at the end of September or beginning of October, the blackberries won't be worth picking, so make the most of them in early October or use any surplus stored in the freezer.

500 g (1 lb 2 oz) apples
150 ml (4 fl oz) water
6 cloves
1.1 kg (2 lb 6 oz) sugar
1 kg (2 lb) blackberries

For hints and tips on jam making, see Seville Orange Marmalade, pp. 26–7.

Peel, core and chop the apples. The size you chop the apples into depends on whether they are cookers or eaters – cookers will dissolve to a pulp, while eaters will retain most of their shape.

Put the apples, water and cloves into a large pot and bring to the boil. Turn down the heat and simmer until soft, about 15 minutes. Meanwhile, put the oven on to GM1/140°C/285°F and put the sugar in to warm up in a heatproof bowl. Put a saucer in the freezer.

When the apples are soft, add the blackberries and stir well. As the blackberries release their juice, add the warm sugar and stir until it has dissolved. Bring to the boil and boil, stirring often, until the setting point is reached (20–25 minutes). When you take the sugar out of the oven, put the jars and their lids in to warm and sterilise.

To test the jam for setting point, put a small spoonful of jam onto the saucer from the freezer and put it into the fridge to cool for a minute or two. Push your finger into the cooled jam from the edge. If it wrinkles, the jam is ready; if not, test again after 5 minutes.

When the jam is ready, take the pot off the heat and leave to cool for 5 minutes. Using a small jug or a ladle, fill the hot jars with the jam. Cover with the lids while hot or with wax discs and cellophane.

sloe gin

Sloes are the fruit of the blackthorn tree, which flowers before the hawthorn or May blossom. It was used along with hawthorn as a thorny hedge to keep livestock in before electric fences were invented. Ideally you should wait for the first frost before picking your sloes, but the birds might get to them before you. So gather ye sloes, while ye may, in October.

If you are feeling thrifty, after the sloe gin has been drained off the sloes, top up the sloes with some dry cider and chill. The sloes give the cider a pale pink colour and a unique flavour, but beware, it has quite a kick.

sloes
sugar
gin

Measure the sloes into a jug. Prick the sloes several times with a skewer and put into a bottle or jar. Measure an equal volume of sugar into the jar with the sloes (if you are using a bottle, pour the sugar through a funnel with a skewer down the centre of it to keep the sugar moving).

Pour an equal volume of gin in and put on the lid. Give it a good shake every day until all the sugar has dissolved, and then leave it until Christmas. Pour off the liquor into a clean bottle. Drink with caution. Makes twice the volume of the gin added.

november

garden

After the clocks have gone back, the garden is a less inviting place. And it can get very cold. But the odd thing is that there are still some jobs to be done which will deliver a bounty in the spring.

Garlic is very easy to grow. Just take a bulb and divide it into cloves and plant each one four inches deep and six inches apart. But don't use ones from the supermarket – if it's not organic, the chances are that it was chemically treated to stop it from sprouting, and even if it is organic, it may not be a variety suited to our climate.

Garlic likes a period of serious cold before it sets about reproducing, so it makes sense to plant it in time to catch the frosty weather. It likes sandy, well-drained soil with plenty of organic matter and will have produced decent bulbs by the time its foliage (which looks similar to leeks) dies in late summer the following year.

The other crop that's worth getting into the ground now is the broad bean. Choose a winter hardy variety and, with a bit of luck, the seeds will germinate and the plants will grow sufficiently before the really cold weather sets in. It's debatable how much is to be gained by sowing in November rather than February, but it may be as much as three weeks, all going well, which means broad beans in May rather than June.

Our little medlar tree represents a tradition that has all but died out. Medlars were popular until the nineteenth century, but they are essentially a medieval fruit, and a strange one, too. After the pretty white flowers appear in the spring, small fruit appear over the summer, which reach the size of a ping pong ball. They are very dense and hard and remain inedible until the flesh has 'bletted', usually by the end of November. This means that the flesh has started to rot, turning soft and brown. You can eat them with a spoon – like you would a kiwi fruit – and the flavour is a cross between a fresh fig and an over-ripe apple. We like to make medlar jelly, which is good on toast or with cold meat.

recipes

November is winter and the evenings are darkening by the day. It's also time to start thinking about Christmas and what seeds to order for next year. Hallowe'en marks the transition into winter. We have the stored fruits of the summer harvest and the autumn seeds and fruits to see us through to spring. Stews and soups reappear on the menu.

beetroot soup

Serves 4-6

Good stock is vital to any soup, as it gives the soup its supporting flavours and lets the main ingredients shine through. For this soup, we add lots of garlic to the stock, but none to the soup. If we were using a chicken stock it would be from a plain chicken, not one that had a lot of tarragon or ginger with it.

1 large onion

1 carrot

2 sticks of celery

2 tbsp oil

100 g (4 oz) bacon pieces*

1–2 beetroots

750 ml (1 pint 5 fl oz) stock

4 tbsp green lentils*

salt and pepper

6 scallions, chopped

sour cream

*The bacon and/or lentils make this soup a meal in itself, and can be left out for a lighter soup to start a meal with.

Peel and slice the onion into very thin half rings. Peel and finely dice the carrot and chop the celery into similar-sized dice. Heat the oil in a large saucepan and add the onion, carrot, celery and bacon. Soften together, but don't brown.

Peel the beetroot and grate it into the saucepan with the onion, etc. Add the stock and bring to the boil. Add the lentils at this stage and simmer until the beetroot and lentils are cooked. Taste and adjust seasoning as necessary.

Finely chop the scallions. Serve the soup topped with a dollop of sour cream and a sprinkling of chopped scallions.

beetroot and orange salad

Serves 4

We find that this is best served while the beetroot is still slightly warm.

2 fresh beetroots

2–3 oranges

salt and pepper

3 tbsp olive oil

6 mint leaves

Put 6 cm (2 inches) of water into the bottom of a steamer pot and put it on a high heat to boil. Wash the beetroots, and if there are any leaves, save the smallest and best to add to the salad. Trim the hairy roots from the beetroots. Put the beetroots into a steamer basket and put it over the boiling water. Turn the heat down to medium so that it continues to steam, but not boil ferociously. Steam the beetroots until they are tender. This will depend on their age and size.

While the beetroots are cooking, cut the skins from the oranges with a sharp knife. Do this on a board or plate that will catch the juice. Cut off any of the membrane that is left from the oranges and slice into rounds.

When the beetroots are cooked, peel (it's best to do this with a knife and fork or wearing rubber gloves if you don't want pink fingers) and slice into rounds. Place alternate slices of beetroot and orange onto a plate and season with salt and pepper. Garnish with the beet leaves around the edge.

Mix the collected orange juice with the oil and pour over the salad. Slice the mint into thin ribbons, sprinkle over the top and serve.

celeriac remoulade

Serves 4

This salad of raw celeriac coated in a mustardy mayonnaise is brilliant with cold roast beef or as a starter with some Parma ham wrapped round it. If you are making your own mayonnaise (see p. 123), add the Meaux mustard when you add the lemon juice halfway through adding the oil.

1 large or 2 small celeriacs

juice of ½ lemon

1 heaped tsp Meaux mustard or any wholegrain mustard

2–3 tbsp mayonnaise

Peel the celeriac and cut into matchstick-size pieces. If your food processor comes with a disk to cut skinny chips, you can use this to cut up the peeled celeriac. Mix the celeriac with the rest of the ingredients in a bowl and season with salt and pepper to taste.

colcannon

Serves 6

This is as traditional as you can get for Hallowe'en. Coins are added to colcannon for good luck.

When it is made well with good spuds, kale that hasn't been overcooked and scallions, it's great. This is a treat and an antidote to all the many flavours and fusion dishes competing for our attention. Serve it with some plain grilled chops or a piece of boiled bacon and give your palate a well-earned rest.

600 g (1 lb 5 oz) potatoes
1 bunch or bag of curly kale
1 bunch of scallions
100 ml (4 fl oz) milk
salt and pepper
70 g (3 oz) butter

Peel and wash the potatoes. Cover with water in a pot and a good pinch of salt. Bring to the boil and cook until a knife can go into the centre of a potato easily.

Meanwhile, wash the kale and remove the central stalks. Cut the leaves into narrow ribbons. Place in the top of a steamer and put 6 cm (2 inches) of water into the bottom. Bring to the boil and steam for 4–5 minutes. (Alternatively, you can steam the kale over the potatoes.)

Cut the roots off the scallions and cut into $\frac{1}{2}$ cm ($\frac{1}{4}$ inch) lengths. Put these into a small saucepan with the milk, a pinch of salt and some pepper. Bring to the boil.

When the potatoes are cooked, drain off the water and mash in the pot with half the butter and some pepper. Beat in the milk and scallions and then add the kale. Stir in well.

Pile the colcannon onto a plate and shape into a mountain. Make a hollow in the top and put in the rest of the butter.

new world coddle

Serves 4

This is really a pumpkin-based stew which, although it contains ingredients from the Americas, reminds us of good old Dublin coddle.

4 short chorizo sausages

3 onions

4 cloves of garlic

1 pumpkin, peeled and chopped into 3 cm (1 inch) cubes

400 g (14 oz) can of chickpeas

1 heaped tsp smoked Spanish paprika

salt and pepper

570 ml (1 pint) stock

small bunch of fresh coriander

Slice the chorizo into 1 cm (¹/₂ inch) slices and place in a large saucepan over a low heat. Peel and thinly slice the onions and garlic and add to the pan. Stir. Turn up to a moderate heat and cook until the onions are softening.

Add the pumpkin and chickpeas to the pan and season with paprika, salt and pepper. Pour in the stock and turn up the heat. Bring to the boil and stir well. Turn down the heat and simmer for about 30 minutes, or until the pumpkin is tender.

Chop the coriander and sprinkle over the soup before serving.

chard and feta flatbreads

Makes 10

When we went to Australia we found these stuffed flatbreads at some of the Sydney weekend markets. There they used spinach instead of chard, and also used a spicy minced meat sauce as a filling. We use the simmering plate of the Aga to cook them on. The leftover central ribs of the chard can be stir-fried.

1 level tsp dried yeast

¼ tsp sugar

300 ml (10 fl oz) hand-hot water

1 tsp salt

500 g (1 lb 2 oz) strong white flour

300 g (10 oz) chard greens

300 g (10 oz) soft goat's cheese or feta cheese

salt and pepper

olive oil

lemon wedges

Mix the yeast, sugar and some of the warm water in a cup and leave in a warm place to froth. Add the salt to the rest of the water and keep warm. Weigh out the flour and sift it into a bowl (warm the bowl first if your house is on the cool side).

The yeast is ready when it has a head like a pint of stout. Pour the yeast into the flour and rinse out the cup with some of the warm water, then pour into the flour, adding the rest of the water. Flours vary in the amount of water they need; you may need more or less than the amount given here. Mix in the water and start to knead the dough, either in a mixer with a dough hook or by hand. Keep kneading until the dough is smooth and springy.

Take the dough out of the bowl and pour a tablespoon of oil into the bowl. Put the dough back in and smear with oil. Cover the bowl and leave to rise. The time taken to rise depends on temperature – 60–90 minutes somewhere warm or all day somewhere cooler.

When the dough has doubled in size and has a domed top, it's ready to use. Divide the dough into 10 evenly sized pieces of dough and on a floured surface, gently knead into balls. Dust with flour and leave to rest for 10–15 minutes.

Shred the chard greens into thin ribbons and break up the cheese. Put a heavy frying pan on to heat or heat up the flat grill plate on a barbecue.

Roll a ball of dough into a thin rectangle with a rolling pin and cover half with one-tenth of the chard (about 30 g/1 oz) and top it with one-tenth of the cheese. Season with salt and pepper. Fold the empty half of the dough over the chard and cheese and squeeze the edges to seal them.

Pour a little oil onto the hot pan or grill plate and put in the dough parcel. Cook on one side until browned, then turn over to cook the other side, 2–3 minutes each side. Lower the heat of the pan if they are browning too fast. Repeat with the rest of the dough, chard and cheese. Cut the hot flatbreads into 4 to 6 pieces and serve with wedges of lemon.

stir-fried chard

Serves 4

We suspect bok choy and Swiss chard are related somewhere along the line, but this is a cookery book, not a botany lesson, so we'll stick to food. The mid-ribs need more cooking time than the green leafy edges, so you get two vegetables for the price of one, so to speak. Or just use the mid-ribs if you have them left over from the Chard and Feta Flatbreads (pp. 220–2). This is particularly good with buckwheat noodles and the pork belly on p. 224.

8–10 leaves of Swiss chard

1 small onion

1 green chilli

2 tbsp oil

2 tbsp soy sauce

black pepper

Wash and dry the chard. Separate the white mid-ribs from the greens. Cut the mid-ribs into thin strips about 7 cm (3 inches) long and shred the greens. Halve and thinly slice the onion. Slice the chilli into thin circles.

Heat the oil in a wok and stir-fry the onion and chilli for a minute, then add the mid-ribs. Put the lid on and cook for a minute or two, then add the greens and stir again. Add the soy sauce and some coarsely crushed black pepper and serve.

roast pork belly with chinese spices

Serves 4

With a pot of brown rice and some stir-fried or steamed greens, these strips of pork belly have a warm, spicy flavour. We sometimes add a chilli for extra heat, but generally the ginger and garlic provide enough. A half teaspoon of ground Sichuan pepper will give an extra depth to the flavours.

8 slices of pork belly 2 cm (³/₄ inch) thick with their rinds on

juice of ¹/₂ lemon

2 tsp Chinese five spice powder

2 tbsp soy sauce

4 cloves of garlic

3 cm (1 inch) piece of ginger

pepper

Put the pork into a bowl and add the lemon juice, five spice powder and soy sauce. Peel the garlic and ginger, chop the garlic and grate the ginger, and add to the pork. Season with pepper and mix the whole lot together. Leave to marinate for as long as you can; even 30 minutes will help. Heat the oven to GM6/200°C/400°F.

Lay the pork strips flat in a single layer in a steel, enamel or ceramic roasting tin or dish. Pour over the liquid from the marinade. Roast for 45 minutes, then turn over the pieces of pork and finish roasting for another 15–25 minutes, depending on how crispy you like pork rinds.

december

garden

Does anyone do much in the garden during December? We certainly don't, although if there's time, it's good to clear the polytunnel of all the withered tomato and aubergine plants and perhaps dig in some manure. After all, the soil here is intensively cultivated and it needs even more feeding than we manage to give it.

Between Christmas and New Year, when the world slows down for us, there is usually the opportunity to review the growing year with the aid of the garden diaries that I keep in a rather patchy fashion.

Odd as it may seem, it's interesting to flick back through the pages and see when the first of each crop was ready for harvesting. But the real value in this little exercise is in helping to decide which varieties to keep growing and which to ditch in favour of something yet to be tried and, from time to time, deciding that certain vegetables may not be worth it, like celery or swedes.

The garden appears either ragged or bare, depending on where you look, but surveying it in the thin winter light gives an opportunity to plan some kind of crop rotation. It's important to avoid growing the same plant, or even members of the same plant family, in the same place year after year. This is because pests and diseases will build up in the soil over time and, indeed, some of the nutrients will get scarce.

A proper crop rotation is hard to manage, but our policy – and it's far from perfect – is to avoid growing the same stuff on the same patch for two years. The only problem lies with the vast brassica family, which includes, to name a few, cabbage, sprouts, broccoli, rocket, turnips, cress and kale. Rotating brassicas is beyond us, but, thankfully, they all seem to grow well. So far.

The seed catalogues will arrive soon and, once again, we will order too much and some packets will reach their expiry dates before we can even think of sowing the contents. That's just one of the imperfections of our kitchen garden. There are plenty of others, but the results are generally satisfactory and as the year draws to its close, we know that growing your own is not one of life's more arduous tasks.

Mind you, there will be lots of digging to be done over the next couple of months and dry weather won't always coincide with the times when we actually want to get out there and wield the spade. But when it does, it can be curiously satisfying. It's the first step in the growing process.

recipes

December is all about getting ready for Christmas and clearing the decks for the New Year. Christmas present lists will contain requests for plants, trees and garden tools. Brassicas reign in the kitchen; cabbages, kale, cavalo nero, Brussels sprouts and the first of an early purple sprouting broccoli, 'Rudolph'. There are good leeks, carrots, beetroot and celery too. There is as much choice in the garden and polytunnel at this time of year as there was in the summer, but it's a different range of vegetables.

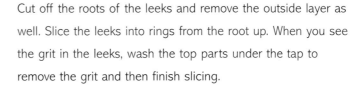

leek and potato soup

Serves 4

Leeks come into their own in mid-winter, thanks to their remarkable hardiness. Combined with potatoes and good stock, they make one of the great soups, simple but brilliant after all the feasting of Christmas.

600 g (1 lb 5 oz) leeks
3 tbsp oil
700 g (1 lb 8 oz) potatoes
300 ml (10 fl oz) water
1 tsp salt
300 ml (10 fl oz) milk or stock

Cut off the roots of the leeks and remove the outside layer as well. Slice the leeks into rings from the root up. When you see the grit in the leeks, wash the top parts under the tap to remove the grit and then finish slicing.

Heat the oil in a saucepan over a medium heat and add the leeks. Stir well to coat with oil and cook until soft. While the leeks are cooking, wash and peel the potatoes. Cut into small pieces about ½ to 1 cm (½ inch) square. Put the potato into the pot with the leeks. Add the water and salt. Turn up the heat and stir well. Bring to the boil, turn down the heat and simmer for about 20 minutes, or until the potato is soft.

Take the pot off the heat and add the milk or stock. Purée the soup in a blender in batches and transfer to a clean pot. Reheat to boiling and serve.

red cabbage and apple

Serves 6–8

Apple sauce is the traditional accompaniment to roast goose and this turns the apples and cabbage into an all-in-one vegetable dish. It's also very good served hot with smoked mackerel.

1 red cabbage, about 600 g (1 lb 5 oz)

juice of ½ lemon

60 ml (2 fl oz) water

2 medium cooking apples, about 600 g (1 lb 5 oz)

3–4 onions, about 300 g (10 oz)

20 g (1 oz) butter

1 tsp caraway seeds

salt and pepper

Set the oven to GM2/150°C/300°F.

Discard the outer leaves of the cabbage and cut it into quarters. Remove the central stalk and slice the rest as thinly as you can. Put the lemon juice into a bowl with the water. Peel, core and thinly slice the apples. As you slice the apples, add them to the water and lemon juice. Peel, halve and slice the onions.

Melt the butter in a heavy casserole over a low heat. Put a layer of cabbage into the casserole, followed by a layer of apple and then onion. Season every onion layer with some caraway seed, salt and pepper.

When all the ingredients are used, pour over the last of the water and lemon juice. Cover the top of the casserole with buttered greaseproof paper and a lid. Turn up the heat and bring the contents to the boil. Pop it in the oven for about 2 hours.

carrot and ginger salad

Serves 4–6

This is a spicy raw chutney, great with curries or cold meat. It's a cold dish, but the spices are warming. A real winter salad.

1 tsp whole cumin seeds

1 tsp black mustard seeds

3 carrots

1 lime

2 cm (¾ inch) piece of fresh ginger

1 large shallot

Put the cumin and mustard seeds into a dry pan and toast on a low heat until they start to change colour and pop. Remove from the heat and leave to cool.

Wash and peel the carrots. Coarsely grate the carrots into a bowl. Squeeze the lime and pour the juice onto the carrots. Peel the ginger and grate over the carrot. Peel and finely slice the shallot into rings and sprinkle over the carrots and ginger. Add the cooled seeds and toss everything together.

Leave to stand for 15–20 minutes to let the flavours blend.

roast root vegetables

This mix of vegetables is a real bung-it-in-the-oven-and-let-it-cook dish. It's great with a roast, chops or with some strong, well-flavoured cheese crumbled into it for the last 10 minutes of its cooking time. The beetroot may need a bit longer if it's on the elderly side. We sometimes have it instead of roast potatoes, as it cooks faster and needs less attention. A big 40 × 28 cm (16 × 11 inch) full roasting dish will feed 6 to 8 people, depending on what else you wish to serve. Our mix depends on what we have in the garden and what we are eating it with.

parsnips
celeriac
Jerusalem artichokes
carrots
beetroot
garlic cloves
shallots or small onions
sprig of thyme
salt and pepper
olive oil

Heat the oven to GM6/200°C/400°F.

Peel and cut the parsnips, celeriac, artichokes, carrots and beetroot into approx. 6 cm (2 inch) chunks. Bruise the cloves of garlic, but don't remove the skin. Peel the shallots or onions.

Put all the vegetables into a roasting dish in a single layer; a few overlaps are allowed, as the vegetables shrink during cooking. Strip the leaves from the thyme stalks and sprinkle over the vegetables, season with salt and pepper and pour over some olive oil. Toss all the vegetables and seasonings together and spread out evenly in the dish. Roast in the oven for 40–60 minutes, rearranging them halfway through.

brussels sprouts

The humble Brussels sprout has been forced into a 'starring' roll at Christmas dinners, and boy, is it a reluctant and seriously shy star. It does not take well to rough or incompetent treatment either, needing to be coaxed and gently encouraged to show its true and sensitive side.

How do we do this? By picking only sprouts the size of large marbles to start with. We then carefully trim any damaged outer leaves off each sprout and cut each one in half. Bring 3 cm (1 inch) of water to the boil in the bottom of a steamer, and when the water is boiling, put the sprouts into the steamer basket and steam for 3–5 minutes, depending on size. They are ready when a dinner fork can be pushed into a half sprout but still have quite a bit of resistance.

Take the steamer off the heat and empty the water out of the bottom. Add a large knob of butter to the bottom of the steamer pan and add the sprouts. Shake the pot well to distribute the butter evenly around the sprouts and serve straight away.

These can be very gently reheated in the pot the next day with any butter still clinging to them. A crisp streaky rasher or two crumbled in gives a nice crunch.

roast goose

Serves 8

Christmas dinner is so hyped, with every magazine, newspaper and daily TV show having a Christmas Cooking Countdown, that for some people it must make moving to a non-Christian country for December seem very appealing.

Christmas dinner is a meal, that's all. Cook within your capabilities and delegate if you're having friends or family. What you choose to eat on this feast day is up to you and your family. If nobody likes turkey, don't cook it. We have cooked a turkey only once and that was the year it actually snowed on Christmas Day. We liked the turkey, but we prefer goose or roast beef. If we're having beef, we abstain from it for two to three weeks before to make it special.

When you get a goose, it may come with a stated weight. Re-weigh it when you have removed the giblets and any loose fat from inside. Sometimes the weight on the goose is the 'dressed' weight by which it is sold and not the final weight. For every 500 g (1 lb 2 oz), it needs to be cooked for 20 minutes, therefore a 5 kg (11 lb) goose will take 3 hours 20 minutes.

Goose produces a lot of fat, which needs to be poured off while it is cooking. A gravy separator is useful for collecting it in, as it means you can save the non-fatty liquid and bits to make the gravy. Goose fat makes the most wonderful roast potatoes. When it's cool, store it in a jar in the fridge for later use. While pouring off the fat during cooking, if the gungy bits are going black, add some boiling water to help with the gravy-making process.

1 goose

Stuffing
150 g (5 oz) breadcrumbs
1 onion
16 sage leaves
salt and pepper
1 small egg

1 small carrot, chopped
1 stick of celery, chopped
1 shallot, chopped
1 small apple, chopped
1 clove of garlic, chopped
sprig of sage

Set the oven to GM6/200°C/400°F.

With a sharp skewer or sharp carving fork, prick the skin of the goose all over; try not to prick the meat under the skin. To make carving easier, remove the wishbone at the neck end of the goose, leaving the skin intact for the stuffing. The wishbone can be removed using a small sharp knife to cut it away from the carcass.

Put the breadcrumbs into a bowl. Peel and finely chop the onion. Cut the sage leaves into narrow ribbons. Add the onion and sage to the breadcrumbs and season with salt and lots of pepper. Break the egg into the breadcrumbs mixture and mix. Stuff the flap of skin at the neck end of the goose and secure the skin around it with cocktail sticks underneath.

Put the wishbone into the cavity of the goose with the chopped carrot, celery, shallot, apple, garlic and the sprig of sage. Chop up the neck if it came with the giblets and put it in the bottom of a deep roasting tin.

Put the goose onto a rack over the roasting tin. Season the outside of the goose with salt and pepper. Pour a glass of water or wine (and one for yourself) into the goose. Put the goose into the hot oven and roast away.

Pour off the fat after 45 minutes and turn the goose round, repeating every hour or so. Each time you pour off the fat, add half a cup of boiling water to the roasting tin so that the gungy bits don't burn. If towards the end of cooking the wings and legs seem to be getting over-browned, cover them with foil.

When the goose is cooked, take it out of the oven. Lift it off the rack and hold it up so that the vegetables and juices from the cavity fall into the roasting tin. Put the goose onto a warm carving dish and keep warm.

Add any of the liquid and bits that were at the bottom of the goose fat that was poured off during the cooking of the goose to the roasting tin and put it on a low heat. Scrape up the bits from the bottom of the tin, adding some more water if it's a bit dry.

When it begins to boil, strain it all into a saucepan and leave it to settle for a few minutes. Pour off the fat and then add a teaspoon of arrowroot or corn flour slaked in some cold water to the gravy. Return to the saucepan and bring to the boil. Simmer to thicken. Taste and season if necessary.

potted goose

Eating up Christmas leftovers shouldn't be the black cloud on the horizon of a tenderly prepared Christmas dinner. We minimise this by having a roast goose, which is good cold the next day, and any left after that gets turned into potted goose. We keep one or two ramekins in the fridge for eating over the next week and the rest go into the freezer for use at a later date.

goose fat
remains of the goose
salt and pepper
bay leaf

Set the oven to GM3/170°C/340°F.

Put whatever goose fat you have into a heavy casserole and put on a low heat. Using your hands, remove the meat from the carcass of the goose and put the meat into the fat. Break the meat into evenly sized pieces, but don't cut it up. Sprinkle the meat with salt and coarse black pepper and add the bay leaf.

Mix together. When it begins to bubble, put the lid on the casserole and into the oven for 45–60 minutes. It's ready when you can separate the fibres of the meat easily with two forks.

Scoop the meat out onto a plate. Strain the goose fat through a sieve into a jar to remove any bits of pepper and the bay leaf left in the fat. Shred the goose meat with two forks and pack into ramekins with a spoonful or two of the goose fat for lubrication. Pack the meat down well to prevent air bubbles forming. Leave them to cool in the fridge and top up with a little more goose fat to seal them, if necessary. Spread dollops onto good toasted bread.

mince pies

Makes 24

We start to want these about two weeks before Christmas to get us into the seasonal mood.

Flaky pastry
250 g (9 oz) plain flour
185 g (6 oz) very cold butter
150–160 ml (5 fl oz) cold water

500 g (1 lb 2 oz) mincemeat (see p. 201)
icing sugar

Sift the flour into a bowl. Cut the butter into small cubes about 1 cm ($\frac{1}{2}$ inch) square and gently stir into the flour. Pour in the cold water and mix to a stiff dough with a knife. Shape into a rough rectangle, wrap and leave to cool in the fridge for 30 minutes.

Remove from the fridge and put onto a floured surface. Roll out into a 1 cm ($\frac{1}{2}$ inch) thick rectangle with a floured rolling pin. Fold the pastry in three and turn so that the three layers are towards you and roll out again, fold in three again, turn, roll and fold again. Wrap and leave in the fridge for 1 hour.

Set the oven to GM7/220°C/425°F.

Cut the pastry into a two-thirds piece and a one-third piece. Roll out the two-thirds piece until it is about 3 mm ($\frac{1}{10}$ inch) thick. Cut into rounds with a 7 cm (3 inch) scone cutter and use these to line 24 bun tins. Gather up the scraps of pastry into layers and set aside. Roll out the other third of the pastry and cut out 24 stars or 7 cm (3 inch) rounds.

Put about 1 teaspoon of mincemeat into each of the pastry cases, depending on how deep the bun tins are; the mincemeat does tend to bubble up and leak out if there's too much.

Dampen the edges of the pastry and top each pie with a star or a round lid. Seal the edges of the round-topped ones and poke a hole in the top with a knife. Paint the tops with beaten egg and bake for 15–20 minutes. If using an Aga, put the tins onto the second set of runners in the roasting oven and bake for 10–15 minutes. Sprinkle over some icing sugar to decorate.

profiteroles

Serves 6

Our children don't like Christmas pudding or mince pies and on Christmas Day these profiteroles go down with the greatest of ease.

Choux paste
60 g (2 oz) butter
150 ml (5 fl oz) water
75 g (3 oz) plain flour
2 medium eggs

300 ml (10 fl oz) cream

Set the oven to GM6/200°C/400°F.

To make the choux paste, put the butter and water into a saucepan and put on a low heat. Sift the flour onto a sheet of paper. When the butter has melted, bring the butter and water mixture to the boil, then add all the flour in one go, beating it in with a wooden spoon.

Icing

60 g (2 oz) Maya Gold chocolate

30 g (1 oz) butter

120 g (4½ oz) icing sugar

2 tbsp water

Take the pan off the heat and keep mixing. When it has cooled for a couple of minutes, add one of the eggs and beat like mad again until the mixture leaves the sides of the pan. Now add the other egg and beat again. The mix should be smooth and glossy.

Lightly grease two baking sheets and put dessertspoonfuls of the mix on about 2 cm (¾ inch) apart. Bake for about 20–30 minutes. Cut the sides with a knife and return to the cooling oven to dry out. Cool on a wire rack.

Whip the cream. To make the icing, melt the chocolate and butter in a bowl over hot water and sift in the icing sugar. Stir in the water and keep stirring until the sauce is smooth.

Split open the profiteroles and fill with whipped cream. Pile onto a plate and pour over the chocolate icing. We make 15 with this amount of choux paste, which means three each, but you can make smaller or larger profiteroles to make more or less. Smaller ones will cook in less time.

index

Amarone risotto, 40
apples, 149, 188
  blackberry and apple jam, 204–5
  blackberry and apple pie, 180–81
  Christmas mincemeat, 201, 240–42
  red cabbage and apple, 230
  Waldorf salad, 194
artichokes, globe
  cooking, 140
  growing, 132
artichokes, Jerusalem
  artichoke soup with rosemary, 56
  growing, 55
  roast, 233
  stoved artichokes, 66
Asian salad dressing, 100–101
asparagus
  cooking, 115
  growing, 114–15
aubergines
  aubergine and yoghurt purée, 175
  aubergine parmigiano, 173–4
  aubergines with pesto, 157
  growing, 12, 53, 71
  vegetable fritters, 155–6

bacon
  coddle, 68
  loin of bacon with parsley sauce, 48–9
  risotto, 16
barbecues, 142
  leg of lamb, 142–3
basil, 131
  pesto, 157
  tomato salads, 135, 136
  vegetable fritters, 156
batter, 155
beans *see* broad beans; French beans

beef
  beef stew with cobbler topping, 103–4
  bolognese, 159
  roast beef, 196–8
  shepherd's pie, 200
beetroot
  beetroot and orange salad, 214
  beetroot cake, 202
  beetroot, carrot and chard stir-fry, 20
  beetroot soup, 213
  roast, 233
black butter, 67
blackberries, 168
  blackberry and apple jam, 204–5
  blackberry and apple pie, 180–81
blackcurrants, 132–3
  blackcurrant jam, 146
blue cheese and walnut salad, 21
blue cheese salad dressing, 101
bolognese, 159
bread
  chard and feta flatbreads, 220–21
  crostini, 171–2
  potato bread, 42–3
broad beans
  broad bean soup, 96
  byessar, 117
  growing, 36–7, 211
broccoli
  growing, 53–4, 113
  purple sprouting broccoli and hollandaise, 64–5
Brussels sprouts
  cooking, 234
  growing, 53–4, 94
buns: hot cross buns, 84–5
butter: black butter, 67
byessar, 117

cabbage
    caldo verde, 59
    cavolo nero and pine nut sauce for pasta, 97
    growing, 53–4, 94, 187–8
    red cabbage and apple, 230
Caesar salad, 102
cakes
    beetroot cake, 202
    orange cake, 25
    summer birthday cake, 127
caldo verde, 59
capers, 121
    black butter, 67
    potato salad with radish and capers, 123
carrots
    beetroot, carrot and chard stir-fry, 20
    carrot and ginger salad, 232
    growing, 36, 53, 72, 131
    roast, 233
casseroles
    beef stew with cobbler topping, 103–4
    lamb arm stew, 177
    lamb hot pot, 82
cavolo nero, 187–8
    cavolo nero and pine nut sauce for pasta, 97
celeriac
    celeriac remoulade, 216
    celeriac salt, 187
    celeriac soup, 190
    growing, 71, 131, 149, 187
    roast, 233
celery
    growing, 71, 131
    roast tomato and celery soup, 154–5
    Waldorf salad, 194
champ, 61
chanterelles, 168
chard, 150
    beetroot, carrot and chard stir-fry, 20

cavolo nero and pine nut sauce for pasta, 97
    chard and feta flatbreads, 220–21
    stir-fried chard, 222
cheese
    Amy's cheesy leek bake, 78
    aubergine parmigiano, 173–4
    blue cheese and walnut salad, 21
    blue cheese salad dressing, 101
    chard and feta flatbreads, 220–21
    cheese sauce, 77
    leeks wrapped in prosciutto, 76–7
    onion and goat's cheese pizza, 178–9
    pesto, 157
    pumpkin and feta quiche, 62
    pumpkin pizza, 17–18
    toasted goat's cheese with winter salad leaves, 45
chicken
    chicken and leek pie, 79–81
    chicken noodle soup, 14–15
    chicken with 40 cloves of garlic, 23
    stock, 14
chocolate icing, 243
chorizo sausages
    caldo verde, 59
    New World coddle, 219
choux paste, 242–3
Christmas mincemeat, 201
    pies, 240–42
chutney
    elderberry chutney, 184
    hints and tips, 26–8
cobbler topping, 104
coddle, 68
    New World coddle, 219
colcannon, 217
compost, 3
cookers, 5
cordial: elderflower cordial, 109
coriander, 124

courgettes
  courgette and herb frittata, 120
  crostini, 171
  flowers, 115, 156
  growing, 53, 71, 92–3
  vegetable fritters, 155–6
crop rotation, 227
crostini, 171–2
crumble
  plums with hazelnut crumble, 162
  rhubarb crumble, 83
crystallised primroses, 87
cucumbers
  cucumber salad, 137
  gazpacho, 134
  growing, 53, 71
  sandwiches, 133
  tomato and cucumber salad, 138
  tzatziki, 139
currants, 132–3
  blackcurrant jam, 146
  redcurrant tartlets, 144–5

desserts
  blackberry and apple pie, 180–81
  gooseberry and elderflower fool, 105
  lemon sauce pudding, 24
  plums with hazelnut crumble, 162
  profiteroles, 242–3
  redcurrant tartlets, 144–5
  rhubarb crumble, 83
digging, 12, 228
dips
  aubergine and yoghurt purée, 175
  byessar, 117
  pesto, 157
  tomato salsa, 158
  tzatziki, 139
drinks
  elderflower cordial, 109
  Granny's lemonade, 31
  orangeade, 29

sloe gin, 207

eggs
  courgette and herb frittata, 120
  parsley and scallion omelette, 39
  salad Niçoise, 141
elderberry chutney, 184
elderflowers
  elderflower cordial, 109
  gooseberry and elderflower fool, 105

feta cheese
  chard and feta flatbreads, 220–21
  pumpkin and feta quiche, 62
filo pastry: pumpkin filo pastry parcels, 191
fish, 5
  gremolata-topped fish fillets, 46
  hake with stewed peppers, 195
  ray/skate with black butter, 67
  smoked haddock supper, 176
flatbread: chard and feta flatbreads, 220–21
French beans
  growing, 54
  salad Niçoise, 141
  vegetable fritters, 155–6
French onion soup, 170
frittata: courgette and herb frittata, 120
fritters: vegetable fritters, 155–6

garlic
  chicken with 40 cloves of garlic, 23
  gremolata-topped fish fillets, 46
  growing, 211
  roast, 233
  wild garlic, 118–19
gazpacho, 134
gem store squashes with tarragon cream,
  192–3
gin: sloe gin, 207
ginger
  carrot and ginger salad, 232
  rhubarb and ginger jam, 86

globe artichokes
  cooking, 140
  growing, 132
goat's cheese
  onion and goat's cheese pizza, 178–9
  pumpkin pizza, 17–18
  toasted goat's cheese with winter salad
    leaves, 45
goose
  potted goose, 239
  roast goose, 235–7
gooseberries, 94
  gooseberry and elderflower fool, 105
  gooseberry jam, 106–7
Greek-style salad, 138
gremolata-topped fish fillets, 46

haddock: smoked haddock supper, 176
hake with stewed peppers, 195
hazelnuts: plums with hazelnut crumble,
  162
herbs, 98, 124, 192
hoeing, 2, 132
hollandaise sauce, 65
horseradish sauce, 198
hot cross buns, 84–5
hot pot: lamb hot pot, 82

icing chocolate, 243

jam, 26–8
  blackberry and apple jam, 204–5
  blackcurrant jam, 146
  gooseberry jam, 106–7
  hints and tips, 26–8
  plum jam, 164
  raspberry jam, 182
  rhubarb and ginger jam, 86
  strawberry jam, 128
Jerusalem artichokes
  artichoke soup with rosemary, 56
  growing, 55

roast, 233
stoved artichokes, 66

kale
  caldo verde, 59
  colcannon, 217
kebabs: lamb kebabs, 124

lamb
  barbecued leg of lamb, 142–3
  lamb arm stew, 177
  lamb hot pot, 82
  lamb kebabs, 124
leeks
  Amy's cheesy leek bake, 78
  chicken and leek pie, 79–81
  coddle, 68
  growing, 72, 113
  leek and potato soup, 229
  leeks wrapped in prosciutto, 76–7
lemons
  Granny's lemonade, 31
  gremolata topped fish fillets, 46
  lemon sauce pudding, 24
lettuce
  Caesar salad, 102
  growing, 36, 98–9, 113–14, 132, 149,
    167
  salad Niçoise, 141
  toasted goat's cheese with winter salad
    leaves, 45
loin of bacon with parsley sauce, 48–9

manure, 3
marmalade: Seville orange marmalade,
  26–8
mayonnaise, 123
  celeriac remoulade, 216
  Waldorf salad, 194
medlars, 211
minced meat: shepherd's pie, 200

mincemeat, 201
  Christmas, 201, 240–42
mince pies, 240–42
mint
  pea and mint soup, 116
  tzatziki, 139
mozzarella cheese: aubergine parmigiano, 173–4
mushrooms, 161, 168
  field mushroom sauce, 161

nettle soup, 74
noodles: chicken noodle soup, 14–15

omelettes
  courgette and herb frittata, 120
  parsley and scallion omelette, 39
onions
  coddle, 68
  French onion soup, 170
  growing, 72–3, 131, 132
  onion and goat's cheese pizza, 178–9
  roast, 233
oranges
  beetroot and orange salad, 214
  orange cake, 25
  orangeade, 29
  Seville orange marmalade, 26–8

pancakes, 50
parsley
  black butter, 67
  growing, 54
  parsley and scallion omelette, 39
  parsley sauce, 49
  vegetable fritters, 156
parsnips
  growing, 53, 54, 187
  roast, 233
pasta
  bolognese, 159
  cavolo nero and pine nut sauce, 97

field mushroom sauce, 161
pastry
  flaky, 81, 180
  short crust, 62
  sweet, 145
pears, 149, 167
peas
  growing, 36, 54
  pea and mint soup, 116
peppers
  crostini, 171–2
  growing, 12, 53, 149
  hake with stewed peppers, 195
  vegetable fritters, 155–6
pesto, 157
pie, savoury: chicken and leek pie, 79–81
pies, sweet
  blackberry and apple pie, 180–81
  mince pies, 240–42
pine nuts
  cavolo nero and pine nut sauce for pasta, 97
  pesto, 157
pizza
  onion and goat's cheese pizza, 178–9
  pumpkin pizza, 17–18
plums
  plum jam, 164
  plums with hazelnut crumble, 162
pork: roast pork belly with Chinese spices, 224
potatoes
  caldo verde, 59
  champ, 61
  coddle, 68
  colcannon, 217
  growing, 35–6, 54–5, 73, 93
  herby new potato salad, 121
  lamb hot pot, 82
  leek and potato soup, 229
  potato bread, 42–3
  potato salad with radish and capers, 123

potatoes *continued*
  potatoes dauphinoise, 60
  roast potatoes, 198
  salad Niçoise, 141
  shepherd's pie, 260
potted goose, 239
preserves, 26–8 *see also* chutney; jam;
  marmalade
primroses, crystallised, 87
profiteroles, 242–3
prosciutto: leeks wrapped in prosciutto,
  76–7
pudding: lemon sauce pudding, 24
pumpkins
  flowers, 115, 156
  growing, 93
  New World coddle, 219
  pumpkin and feta quiche, 62
  pumpkin filo pastry parcels, 191
  pumpkin pizza, 17–18
  pumpkin soup, 38
  roast pumpkin with cumin, thyme and
    oregano, 41
purple sprouting broccoli and hollandaise,
  64–5

quiche: pumpkin and feta quiche, 62
quinces, 167

radishes
  growing, 54, 150
  potato salad with radish and capers, 123
raspberries, 133, 150
  raspberry jam, 182
ray with black butter, 67
red cabbage and apple, 230
redcurrants, 132–3
  redcurrant tartlets, 144–5
rhubarb, 73
  rhubarb and ginger jam, 86
  rhubarb crumble, 83
risotto, 16

Amarone risotto, 40
  risotto primavera, 118–19
roast beef, roast spuds and horseradish
  sauce, 196–8
roast goose, 235–7
roast pork belly with Chinese spices, 224
rocket, 36, 149
rotation of crops, 227

salad dressings, 99–102
  Asian dressing, 100–101
  blue cheese dressing, 101
  Caesar salad, 102
  mayonnaise, 123
  mustard/garlic dressing, 100
salad leaves
  growing, 36, 98–9, 113–14, 132, 149,
    167
  toasted goat's cheese with winter salad
    leaves, 45
salads
  beetroot and orange, 214
  blue cheese and walnut, 21
  Caesar salad, 102
  carrot and ginger, 232
  celeriac remoulade, 216
  cucumber, 137
  green, 98
  herby new potato, 121
  potato with radish and capers, 123
  salad Niçoise, 141
  tomato, 135, 136
  tomato and cucumber, 138
  Waldorf salad, 194
  see also salad dressings
salsa: tomato salsa, 158
salt, 6–7
sauces
  aubergine and yoghurt purée, 175
  bolognese, 159
  cavolo nero and pine nut sauce for pasta,
    97

cheese sauce, 77
field mushroom sauce, 161
fresh tomato sauce, 138
hollandaise sauce, 65
horseradish sauce, 198
parsley sauce, 49
pesto, 157
tomato salsa, 158
tzatziki, 139
sausages
coddle, 68
see also chorizo sausages
scallions
champ, 61
colcannon, 217
growing, 54, 150
parsley and scallion omelette, 39
smoked haddock supper, 176
vegetable fritters, 155–6
scones: potato scones, 42–3
seasoning, 6–7
shallots
growing, 72, 132
roast, 233
shepherd's pie, 200
skate with black butter, 67
sloe gin, 207
smoked haddock supper, 176
soup
artichoke with rosemary, 56
beetroot, 213
broad bean, 96
caldo verde, 59
celeriac, 190
chicken noodle, 14–15
French onion, 170
gazpacho, 134
leek and potato, 229
nettle, 74
pea and mint, 116
pumpkin, 38
roast tomato and celery, 154–5

spices, 7
spinach *see* chard
squashes
flowers, 115, 156
gem store squashes with tarragon cream,
192–3
growing, 93, 131
stews
beef stew with cobbler topping, 103–4
coddle, 68
coddle, New World, 219
lamb arm stew, 177
see also casseroles
stir-fry
beetroot, carrot and chard stir-fry, 20
stir-fried chard, 222
stock
chicken, 14
vegetable, 38
stoved artichokes, 66
strawberries
growing, 114
strawberry jam, 128
summer birthday cake, 127
stuffing, 236
summer birthday cake, 127
sweetcorn
cooking, 169
growing, 91–2, 149

tarragon cream, 192–3
tartlets, redcurrant, 144–5
tomatoes
aubergine parmigiano, 173–4
bolognese, 159
crostini, 171–2
fresh tomato sauce, 138
gazpacho, 134
growing, 12, 53, 91, 92, 131
roast tomato and celery soup, 154–5
roast tomatoes, 152
salad Niçoise, 141

tomatoes *continued*
   smoked haddock supper, 176
   tomato and cucumber salad, 138
   tomato salads, 135, 136
   tomato salsa, 158
tuna: salad Niçoise, 141
turnips, 53, 54
tzatziki, 139

vegetables
   barbecued, 142–3
   roast root vegetables, 233
   vegetable fritters, 155–6
   see also under individual vegetables

Waldorf salad, 194
walnuts
   blue cheese and walnut salad, 21
   Waldorf salad, 194
watering, 131, 149
weeding, 2, 3, 132

yoghurt: aubergine and yoghurt purée, 175
Yorkshire pudding, 199